MINIMAL CEREBRAL DYSFUNCTION IN CHILDREN

Seminars in Psychiatry

MINIMAL CEREBRAL DYSFUNCTION IN CHILDREN

Edited by

Stanley Walzer, M.D.
Assistant Professor of Psychiatry
Harvard Medical School
Boston, Massachusetts

Peter H. Wolff, M.D.
Professor of Psychiatry
Harvard Medical School
Boston, Massachusetts

GRUNE & STRATTON
New York and London

Minimal Cerebral Dysfunction in Children is reprinted from the February 1973 issue (Volume V, Number 1) of the quarterly journal *Seminars in Psychiatry,* published by Grune & Stratton, Inc.

Library of Congress Cataloging in Publication Data

Walzer, Stanley, comp.
    Minimal cerebral dysfunction in children.

    Includes bibliographies.
    1. Brain-damaged children. I. Wolff, Peter H., joint comp. II. Title
RJ506.M4W34   618.9'28'5884   72-14118
ISBN 0-8089-0798-0

© *1973 by Grune & Stratton, Inc.*

All rights reserved. No part of this publication may be reproduced or transmitted in any form or by any means, electronic or mechanical, including photocopy, recording, or any information storage and retrieval system, without permission in writing from the publisher.

Grune & Stratton, Inc.
111 Fifth Avenue, New York, New York 10003

Library of Congress Catalog Card Number 72-14118
International Standard Book Number 0-8089-0798-0

Printed in the United States of America

MINIMAL CEREBRAL DYSFUNCTION IN CHILDREN

Contents

Introduction .... *Stanley Walzer and Julius B. Richmond*		1
Genetic Issues in the Syndrome of Minimal Brain Dysfunction *Gilbert S. Omenn*		5
Studies of Monkeys Asphyxiated at Birth: Implications for Minimal Cerebral Dysfunction ...... *Jeri A. Sechzer, Maria D. Faro, and William F. Windle*		19
EEG Issues in Children With Minimal Brain Dysfunction ... *James H. Satterfield*		35
Lead Poisoning in Children: Neurologic Implications of Widespread Subclinical Intoxication .... *Herbert L. Needleman*		47
Identification and Diagnosis of Children With Learning Disabilities: An Interdisciplinary Study of Criteria .... *Helmer R. Myklebust*		55
Neurologic and Behavioral Assessment of Children With Minimal Brain Dysfunction .... *B. C. L. Touwen and A. F. Kalverboer*		79
The Hyperkinetic Syndrome .... *John E. O'Malley and Leon Eisenberg*		95
Functional Implications of the Minimal Brain Damage Syndrome *Peter H. Wolff and Irving Hurwitz*		105
Index..		116

Introduction

SCIENTIFIC INQUIRY is directed increasingly to more specific and subtle questions as knowledge accumulates and the tools for investigation sharpen. In the early decades of this century, the biomedical sciences were concerned with life-threatening situations that surrounded and affected man; they had the tools and knowledge available to identify these factors and begin to master them. Now we are ready to focus our investigations on more subtle problems, which, although not life-threatening, do result in a great loss of human potential. We recognize that every child has the right of good health and the right to realize his full potential. With this in mind, we are turning our investigations to those factors that interfere—however minimally—with the realization of the child's full potential, with the aim of minimizing these factors.

It seems natural, then, that interest is now being directed to the issues of minimal brain dysfunction. Furthermore, it becomes increasingly evident that the presence of structural alterations of the brain resulting from anatomic insult cannot be limited to the group of children who demonstrate either gross neurologic deficits or the symptom constellation of hyperkinesis, short attention span, perceptual handicaps, learning disorders, emotional lability, and other behavioral difficulties. The more sophisticated the neurologic assessment procedures, the more prevalent are the signs suggestive of central nervous system impairment. Indeed, we might not find the expected symptom constellation at all, but other behavioral variations, which themselves might not even be recognized as being psychopathologic.

Immediately upon approaching this subject, we encounter the problem of definition and semantics. Some investigators refer to the disorder as minimal cerebral dysfunction, while others call it minimal brain damage or minimal brain dysfunction. Some equate it with learning disabilities, while others see learning disabilities as representing only one facet of the disorder. Terms such as hyperkinesis, specific learning disability, dyslexia, and others are included within the broad designation of minimal brain dysfunction. Clearly, we need a taxonomy for this group of disorders.

In this seminar we attempt to bypass the semantic chaos and present the concept of minimal cerebral dysfunction in a more global way. We are concerned ultimately with the child's psychosocial adaptation—his capacity to use to the fullest his internal and external resources in order to function optimally under any circumstances in which he is placed. The factors and forces that contribute to and shape the total development of the child are complex but intimately related, and are presented in part in Fig. 1. Successful adaptation, however, is possible only when a degree of homeostasis exists among these variables.

The term "minimal cerebral dysfunction" implies structural impairment or alteration of the nervous tissue of the brain. Some of the behavioral manifestations from such an insult are the direct result of the impairment of functions intrinsically related to the central nervous system. However, at a higher level of operation, such structural alterations give the child a unique but impaired nervous system with which to interact with the developmental environment. Behavioral development resulting from such an interaction will be different from that seen in children without such impairment. The capacities of the child for adaptation become limited, and behavioral symptoms representing complex psychosocial maladaptations (i.e., learning disorders) may result. Birch sees such children as "individuals with damage to the nervous system, which may have resulted in some primary disorganization, who have developed patterns of behavior in the course of atypical relations with the developmental environment, including its interpersonal, objective and social features."[1]

With this orientation in mind, any attempt to examine systematically the subject of minimal cerebral dysfunction requires that certain issues be presented. Attention must be paid to the more sophisticated diagnostic approaches that can be employed to identify the presumed structural alteration of the nervous system. Neuroanatomic and neuropathologic processes must also be examined as they relate to the behavioral disturbances. Finally, we must include careful clinical studies of the developmental consequences of the processes (i.e., learning disorders); only then can we develop hypotheses that relate the biologic variation to the more comprehensive and complicated issues of behavioral development as a psychosocial adaptational process.

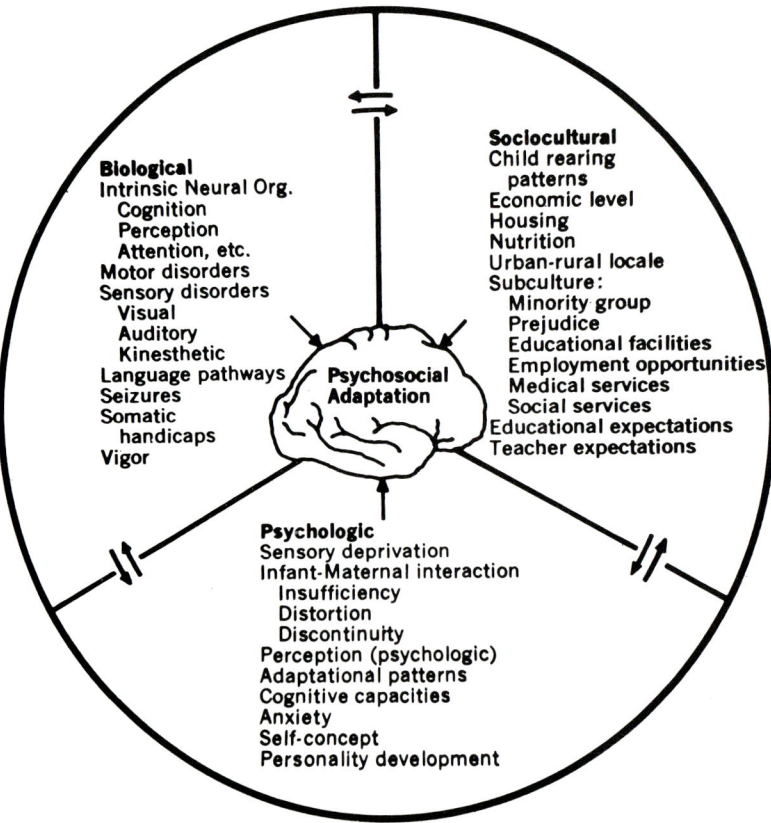

Fig. 1. Multiple factors affecting psychosocial adaptation. (From Richmond, J. B.[2])

INTRODUCTION

In this seminar we present clinical and experimental data that focus both on the issue of brain damage and on the developmental "end products" of the complex interaction between the biologically handicapped child and his surrounding world.

In studying the problem of minimal cerebral dysfunction, two investigative approaches are possible. If we accept the concept that a complex interaction of factors may be involved etiologically and that the psychosocial maladaptation results from the interplay of these variables, studies can be organized from a comprehensive, multifactorial approach. Such studies attempt to find which of the many variables are etiologically or developmentally significant for a broad group of children who manifest a constellation of symptoms associated with minimal brain dysfunction. They might be highly successful ventures that both separate out the specific factors involved and suggest possible etiologic mechanisms that apply for a large number of affected children. Although such studies allow for generalization, they may lack the specificity to define fully a particular facet of the problem.

Another way to proceed would be to focus on a group of children who may be predisposed to minimal brain dysfunction by virtue of specifically defined etiologic factors. Thus, there exists an extensive literature on the developmental consequences of prematurity, low birthweight, various prenatal and perinatal disorders, early exposure to toxins, etc. Alternatively, the investigator might focus on a particular process—such as learning disability—and study some specific variable of interest to him.

The more specific studies such as these provide a large body of important information; some investigators even suggest that it is through such studies rather than through large-scale comprehensive endeavors that we will ultimately learn what we need to know. However, it must be understood that the specific criteria for selection or the limited areas of investigation define a specific population or a specific area of involvement and limit the generalizations that can be made from the results with respect to the general population of children with minimal brain dysfunction.

We have included both styles of investigative approaches in order to emphasize the contribution that each can make to further the knowledge in the complex area of minimal cerebral dysfunction. Comprehensive, multifactorial approaches are presented along with research on more specific factors. We have included experimental, clinical, and epidemiologic studies. Although this volume obviously cannot be all-inclusive, we hope it is representative of the current work and thought in the area of minimal brain dysfunction.

We would particularly like to express our appreciation to Miss Gladys Litter, administrative secretary of the Judge Baker Guidance Center, for immeasurable help in editing the manuscripts.

Stanley Walzer, M.D.
Julius B. Richmond, M.D.

REFERENCES

1. Birch, H. G.: The problem of "brain damage" in children. *In* Birch, H. G. (Ed): Brain Damage in Children. Baltimore, Williams & Wilkins, 1964, p. 8.
2. Richmond, J. B.: Epidemiology of learning disorders. *In* Menkes, J. H., and Schain, R. J. (Eds.): Learning Disorders in Children, Report of the Sixty-First Ross Conference on Pediatric Research. Columbus, Ohio, Ross Laboratories, 1971, p. 14.

Genetic Issues in the Syndrome of Minimal Brain Dysfunction

Gilbert S. Omenn, M.D., Ph.D.

THE DIAGNOSTIC LABEL "Minor Cerebral Dysfunction" or "Minimal Brain Dysfunction" (MBD) has been applied to a category of childhood behavioral disorders that constitutes the majority of referrals to child guidance centers and affects some 5%-15% of school children.[63] The hallmarks of the syndrome are the constellation of core clinical signs—motor hyperactivity, distractibility, impulsivity, and learning performance below that expected from objective tests[9,21,31,56]—and the favorable effect of drugs that are CNS stimulants.[5,6,14] However, the clinical manifestations, birth and general medical history, neurologic and EEG findings, and responsiveness to therapeutic measures are all highly variable.

It is evident to me that two major approaches of medical genetics may be applied fruitfully to clinical and basic studies of MBD.[38] The first approach attempts to establish the extent to which genetic factors are involved in MBD, and to sort the likely heterogeneity into specific entities, with defined etiologic, diagnostic, and prognostic characteristics. The second approach may be termed "psychopharmacogenetics," the analysis of genetically determined differences in metabolism of or response to psychoactive drugs.[39] Such analyses of the responses of individual youngsters with MBD to amphetamines (D- and L-), methylphenidate, and phenobarbital can be combined efficiently with treatment protocols.

ROLE OF GENETIC FACTORS IN MBD

Behavioral disorders are notoriously difficult to evaluate for the relative roles of inherited and environmental factors. When the incidence of a behavioral disorder is demonstrated to be greater among relatives of an affected person than in the general population, methods must be applied to distinguish the effects of shared environment and interpersonal interactions from genetically transmitted biologic effects. Behavioral phenotypes are highly variable clinically and are far removed from the direct effects of single genes and enzymes. A similar phenotype may result from a variety of etiologic mechanisms, which may have very different genetic inputs; and the interaction of a genetic predisposition with environmental stresses may defy detailed analysis. Nevertheless, several epidemiologic methodologies have proved to be instructive (see Table 1). (1) The prevalence of the disorder may vary in different geographic, ethnic, or racial populations. Examples of high prevalence due to restricted gene frequencies are Tay-Sachs disease in Ashkenazic Jews and sickle-cell anemia in blacks. (2) First-degree relatives (parents, siblings, and children) of affected individuals may have a higher risk than the general population of being or becoming affected with the same disorder. Such is the case for epilepsy,[41] depression,[22,65] schizophrenia,[43,44] and

---

Supported by USPHS Grant GM15253, a National Genetics Foundation Fellowship, and Research Career Development Award (GM43122) from the Public Health Service.

Reprint requests should be addressed to Gilbert S. Omenn, M.D., Ph.D., Division of Medical Genetics, Departments of Medicine and Genetics, University of Washington, Seattle, Wash. 98195.

Table 1. Epidemiologic Data Needed for MBD

---
(1) Population frequencies
   With geographic, ethnic, racial, and socioeconomic composition
(2) Frequency in first-degree relatives
   (Parents, siblings, and children of affected patients)
(3) Twin studies (MZ versus DZ concordance)
(4) Adoption studies
   Half-sibs; MZ twins reared apart
   Biologic and adoptive parents and relatives of probands
---

alcoholism.[49] (3) Identical, monozygotic (MZ) twins may be compared with fraternal, dizygotic (DZ) twins.[58] If one twin is affected, the probability that the other is affected (concordant) should be high for MZ twins if genetic factors are important. The concordance in DZ twins would be lower, similar to that for ordinary siblings. The DZ twins must be of the same sex, especially if the frequency of the disorder differs by sex, as in MBD. Conversely, the extent to which MZ twins are discordant is an indication of the influence of environmental factors. (4) In order to distinguish genetic from intrafamilial environmental factors, it is useful to study individuals raised from as early ages as possible by individuals who are not the biologic parents. Such studies include the comparison of MZ twins reared together vs. MZ twins reared apart,[27,51] and comparison of the incidence of a disorder in the biologic vs. the adoptive relatives of affected probands who were adopted early in life[25,44] or who are half-sibs.[49] These methods provide statistical indications of genetic determination of or genetic predisposition to behavioral disorders. Detailed understanding of such inherited predisposition awaits the demonstration of specific metabolic or enzymatic mechanisms.

Epidemiologic data with regard to MBD are limited. However, a few studies have been carried out. First, estimates of population frequencies for MBD have been collected from surveys in Holland, St. Louis (Missouri), Vermont, and Montgomery County (Maryland).[63] The diagnostic bases were minor neurologic signs, teachers' reports of overactivity and short attention span, and school questionnaires. An incidence of approximately 10% for symptomatic cases of "MBD" was found in each study. Boys were much more likely to be affected than girls, with a sex ratio of 4-10 boys to 1 girl, using hyperactivity as a criterion. However, racial and ethnic composition of the affected groups has not been characterized, and little attention has been given to socioeconomic status, another important epidemiologic parameter.

Two studies of the frequency of psychiatric problems and childhood MBD in the relatives of patients with MBD are now available. Morrison and Stewart[36] obtained data from interviews of the parents of 59 children with the hyperactivity syndrome and parents of 41 control children. The controls were surgical patients in the same hospital and were well matched for age of the child, age of both parents, birth order, sibship size, and socioeconomic status. All were white. There was a statistically significant excess of psychiatric diagnoses among the parents of the affected children, with the excess due to alcoholism in both mothers and fathers, hysteria in mothers, and sociopathy in fathers. There was no increased incidence of depression. Review of childhood histories of parents and aunts and uncles indicated a highly significant excess of hyperactive behavior in these relatives of affected children, compared to the control families. Abnormal behavior in parents, aunts, and uncles was found as commonly in families where the affected adult had little or no contact with the child as in families where the hyperactive child had lived with the affected adult. In a similar study, Cantwell[7] interviewed the parents of 50 children with MBD and 50 control children at a military base in California, confirming the excess of alcoholism in mothers and fathers, hysteria in mothers, and sociopathy in fathers of the patients with MBD. Ten parents had childhood histories suggestive of MBD, and all ten had adult psychopathology. Again, there was no excess of affective disorders.

Such family studies focus attention on functionally related types of psychopathology. In performing family studies, the psychiatrist is forced to consider the natural history of a behavioral abnormality. These reports indicate that alcoholism, hysteria, and sociopathy may be importantly related to a history of hyperactivity in childhood, and other evidence suggests that the follow-up of hyperactive children through adolescence and into adulthood reveals continued learning difficulties and tendency to sociopathic behavior, despite disappearance of motor hyperactivity.[34,62] Because of the social importance of such conclusions and because the chronic use of psychoactive drugs must be evaluated with knowledge both of long-term benefits and long-term hazards, much more extensive follow-up data are needed. Also, some infants and preschool children have aberrant behavior patterns with extreme overreactivity, sensitivity, and inattentiveness. At least some of these infants appear to become hyperactive schoolchildren, and many children with MBD have histories of such difficulties beginning at an early age. The earlier a behavioral disorder can be recognized, the more important must be inherited, intrauterine, and neonatal factors, compared to psychodynamic factors in the family.

Several examples of sibships with more than one affected child are known. Sulzbacher[61] has noted two such sibships, with two brothers affected in each, among the patients in Seattle. Wender[63] mentioned several instances of clustering of cases within families, including one sibship with four children diagnosed as MBD and another with four boys having reading difficulties. When familial dyslexia is gathered into the "umbrella" category, the definition of "MBD" may be too inclusive. However, youngsters referred for a combination of hyperactivity and poor learning may have predominant difficulties in arithmetic or in reading, such that the distinctions between MBD and "specific learning disability" are often blurred. Genetic factors appear to be quite important in dyslexia, with an autosomal dominant pattern of transmission from parents to children in many families. The classical study in Scandinavia by Hallgren[24] has been reanalyzed but not duplicated in this country.[16,52,59]

In the third category, studies of twins, I am aware of only a single report. Lopez[33] evaluated 10 pairs of twins, at least one of whom had a hyperactivity syndrome. Four pairs of MZ twins were all concordant, while only one of six DZ pairs was concordant. Unfortunately, four of the six DZ pairs were not of the same sex, with the male affected in three of the four instances. The MZ twins were all boys. Since there is usually a marked excess of boys affected with MBD, much more extensive data with like-sex twin pairs are needed.[48] Large-scale, ongoing twin studies in major city school systems such as Philadelphia[48] and Louisville[64] provide excellent opportunities to assess twin concordance rates for MBD and the effect of socioeconomic status and other measured variables.

Finally, in an unpublished study by Safer[63] of full sibs and half-sibs of 14 MBD children, all reared in foster homes, 50% of the full sibs vs. 14% of the half-sibs had hyperactivity, diagnosed by short attention spans and repeated behavior problems. Neither lower birth weight in the full sibs nor later placement in foster homes for the half-sibs vitiates the conclusion that genetic factors are relatively important. In another case, a 7-yr-old with MBD had been separated at birth from her mother, a chronic schizophrenic.[63]

Morrison and Stewart[37] have studied relatives of adopted children in another attempt to distinguish intrafamilial environmental factors from inherited mechanisms that might account for the increased incidence of psychiatric abnormalities and childhood hyperactivity observed in the families of hyperactive children.[7,36] Although the detailed data have not yet been published, the analyses indicate that there is no excess of psychopathology among the foster families of hyperactive adopted children. These results strongly implicate biologic and inherited factors in the predisposition to behavioral abnormalities classified as MBD. However, these studies do not permit inferences about the exact mechanisms of such genetic effects or about the likely variety or heterogeneity of etiologic processes that could result in the hyperactivity syndrome.

GENETIC HETEROGENEITY: THE EXAMPLE OF MENTAL RETARDATION

Just as hyperactive and impulsive behavior of children with MBD may overlap with the behavior of "normally" active, inquisitive, curious youngsters, the IQs of mentally subnormal or mentally defective children overlap with the Normal (Gaussian) distribution of IQ in a population. Roberts[42] and Penrose[40] have summarized the development of understanding in this field since the 1930s. Cutoff points on the continuum of levels of intelligence in the population have been made arbitrarily, for reasons of educational and legislative administration.[53] Mental subnormality has been divided into two types (see Table 2): (1) a cultural or "physiologic" type, in which the defect is mild and the parents and sibs have below-average intelligence; and (2) a "pathologic," often more severe defect, with parents usually of normal intelligence. The cultural type includes the lower 2% of the general population distribution, while the pathologic type involves about 0.25%. Stanford-Binet IQ tests of 3,361 children in Bath, England[42] gave a distribution with 16-fold excess of individuals below IQ 45. Next, siblings of retarded children were studied. The IQs of sibs of the "feeble-minded" (IQ 45-60) fit a fairly Normal curve, with a mean IQ of 80. The IQs of sibs of "imbeciles" (IQ 35-45) gave a different Normal curve, with a mean IQ of 100, but with a hump at the very lower end, representing similarly affected sibs.[42]

Among children with pathologic mental subnormality, there was little evidence of genetic causation 40-50 yr ago. Affected sibs were uncommon, and affected parents

Table 2. Types of Mental Retardation

	Cultural—Physiologic	Pathologic
Severity	Mild	Usually severe
Other clinical signs	Absent	Often present
Parents' IQ	Below average	Normal
Sibs' IQ	Below average	Usually normal; few very low.
Genetic causes	Polygenic	Rare recessive genes; autosomal chromosomal abnormality (e.g., mongolism)
Environmental causes	Social deprivation; mild exogenous insults	Early cerebral disease or injury
Social class	Increased frequency in lower classes	All social classes
Fertility	Normal, ? increased	Low or absent

were almost never observed (because of impaired fertility). Gradually, specific entities were recognized. Down's syndrome or mongolism was differentiated by its associated clinical signs and then was shown almost 100 yr later to have a specific chromosomal abnormality (trisomy 21). Epidemiologic, clinical, and virologic studies identified maternal rubella (German measles) as a cause of retardation. A chemical test on the urine differentiated phenylketonuria. Extensive screening of chromosome karyotypes and certain metabolic products in tissues and fluids from children in institutions for the mentally retarded has generated a rapidly expanding list of specific, rare conditions that contribute to the frequency of the overall phenotype of mental retardation. Even so, the majority of cases of severe retardation remains "undifferentiated" as to cause, fitting no known syndromes. Of course, intrauterine viral infections, birth injuries, and almost all chromosomal abnormalities occur sporadically. Even with autosomal recessive and X-linked inherited traits, the probability of finding an affected sibling depends on family size and on survival of affected children to be diagnosed. Finally, autosomal dominant causes of mental retardation (tuberous sclerosis, neurofibromatosis, myotonic dystrophy) are highly variable in clinical expression and only the relatively mildly affected individuals have children, so mental retardation is not detected in the parents. Thus, it is not surprising that genetic mechanisms were long obscured by such heterogeneity in the etiology of mental retardation. Furthermore, what may appear from statistical analysis to be polygenic inheritance may, in fact, be the resultant of several different genetic mechanisms, each or many of which are monogenic.

No specific patterns of inheritance have been identified yet in families with MBD. Also, no evidence of aneuploidy of the sex chromosomes (such as XXY) was found in screening of 96 MBD patients (82 boys, 14 girls) for sex chromatin, and no other chromosomal abnormalities were found in complete karyotypes of 23 of these patients.[60]

SEX DIFFERENCE IN FREQUENCY OF MBD: SIGNIFICANCE FOR A POLYGENIC HYPOTHESIS

Marked deviation from equal frequency for diseases in the two sexes is observed commonly in medicine. Among congenital malformations, male:female ratios are 5:1 for pyloric stenosis, 2:1 for talipes equinovarus, 1.5:1 for harelip (± cleft palate), 1:2 for anencephaly, and 1:6 for congenital dislocation of the hip.[8] There is no suggestion that genes on the X chromosome play a direct part in the causation of any of these conditions, and transmission of the disorder (e.g., pyloric stenosis) from affected males to their sons rules out X-linkage. The sex ratio differences presumably reflect effects of hormones on sensitive tissues, especially during prenatal life.

Carter[8] has provided a valuable analysis of the relationship between sex ratio and polygenically determined risks in first-degree relatives. A good example is infantile pyloric stenosis. If untreated, the patient either dies or recovers completely by about age 4 mo. If the genetic predisposition has the same basis in males and females and is multifactorial, the high sex ratio would imply that affected females are more extreme deviants (exceed a higher threshold) than the males. Thus, female probands would be expected to carry more of the abnormal genes making for pyloric stenosis and have a higher incidence in relatives. In Carter's London Series, the proportions of first-degree relatives of male index patients affected with pyloric stenosis were 4.6% for male and

Table 3. Risk of Pyloric Stenosis in Relatives According to Sex*

First-degree Relatives	Male Probands ($n = 281$)	Female Probands ($n = 149$)
Male	4.6% ± 1.0%	15.4% ± 3.1%
Female	2.3% ± 0.7%	9.8% ± 2.4%

*Carter, 1968.

2.3% for female relatives; for relatives of female index patients 15.4% of males and 9.8% of females were affected (see Table 3). These percentages are, respectively, 10, 25, 30, and 100 times the incidences in the same sex in the general population, consistent with the expectations of model of polygenic inheritance. Analogous studies comparing the frequency of MBD in relatives of boys and of girls affected with MBD might be highly informative if polygenic inheritance is involved, because of the high sex ratio.

The higher incidence in males is also interesting in view of studies in man[20,35] and monkeys[23] on the effects of sex hormone exposure during gestation on subsequent sexually dimorphic behaviors. Androgens during pregnancy can influence the psychologic development of girls, as shown both in the adrenogenital syndrome and in cases in which synthetic progestational agents were administered to pregnant mothers to prevent threatened miscarriages. Using criteria of play with boys' toys, athletic energy, outdoor pursuits, and extent of concern for feminine frills, doll play, baby care, and household chores, Money and his colleagues found that nearly all these girls could be considered "tomboys."[20] Conversely, there are genetic males with a normal 46 XY chromosome karyotype who are "insensitive" in their target organs to the effects of testosterone. The disorder, called testicular feminization, is inherited as a single gene effect. These males appear to be normal females at birth and through puberty and come to medical attention in their teens for amenorrhea or infertility or else because of inguinal hernias (with testes in the inguinal canal). Psychologic evaluation of ten such patients showed unmistakably feminine behavior and outlook,[35] confirmed by interview of the husbands of four married patients. Thus, one of the important "target organs" for the sex hormones is the developing nervous system.

From such considerations, the preponderance of boys among children diagnosed as having MBD, therefore, implies nothing about sex-linked inheritance, but does suggest approaches to analysis of family data according to sex of the proband.

PHARMACOGENETIC ANALYSIS OF MBD

In several reports between 1937 and 1950, Bradley[5,6] documented the effectiveness of Benzedrine (D,L amphetamine) and Dexedrine (D-amphetamine) in the treatment of the hyperactivity syndromes and other behavioral disorders of childhood. The excitatory effects of phenobarbital were also recognized 30 yr ago.[32] It is my impression that prompt and dramatic improvement occurs in only a small proportion of cases, that the majority have some or considerable improvement, due at least in part to environmental structuring and placebo-effect, and that some have no response or even become worse. For example, in Conners' data,[11] 23% were "much improved" after 4 wk and 36% after 8 wk on Dexedrine. Another 65% and 41% were rated "improved" at the same times, but 35% and 30% of the group on placebo also were "improved." "Improvement" should signify both decrease in some key parameter of

Fig. 1. Chemical formulas for amphetamine (mol wt = $368 \div 2 = 184$) and methylphenidate (mol wt = 233). Note that each drug has an asymmetric, optically active carbon, so that the potency of its two stereoisomers may be compared.

AMPHETAMINE
(d-α-methylphenethylamine)$_2 \cdot$H$_2$SO$_4$

METHYLPHENIDATE
α-phenyl-2-piperidine acetic acid methyl ester

obnoxious behavior and increase in performance of arithmetic problems or some other appropriate learning skill in school. Obviously, an overall sedative effect is not desired.

The heterogeneity of response to drug therapy makes comparisons across studies very difficult. In factor-analyzing his own data, Conners[12] found IQ score gains and reading improvement in *some* children with dramatic drug effects. Yet, a given test might show increased, decreased, or unchanged performance in different subjects; a certain skill might be improved according to one test, but not when assessed with a different test; some of the most significantly improved functions (figure drawing and Bender-Gestalt design copying) had failed to respond in previous studies; other functions, including auditory synthesis and rote learning, showed no response after a positive result in a previous study. Of course, there are analogous discrepancies in the results of other investigators.

The marked variation in responsiveness to therapy is probably due to heterogeneity of the behavior disorders within and among the different groups of patients. Since some children fail to improve or even get worse on amphetamine,[6] other drugs have been tried. For example, the tricyclic antidepressant imipramine has been reported to be effective in some children unresponsive to D-amphetamine.[66] A number of studies indicate that methylphenidate (Ritalin) is roughly equivalent in its effectiveness to amphetamine,[28] though twice the dose on a per mg basis is advised.[10] Thus, Ritalin (Fig. 1) is approximately 40% as potent as amphetamine on a molar basis (mol wt methylphenidate = 233; mol wt [D-amphetamine]$_2$:H$_2$SO$_4$ = $\frac{368}{2}$ = 184). However, I cannot find any studies in which Ritalin and amphetamine were compared in the same patients. It is quite possible that dual testing of individual patients with Ritalin and amphetamine may reveal clinically useful heterogeneity of response.

Table 4 presents the protocol developed at the Child Development and Mental Retardation Center at the University of Washington for a multidisciplinary clinical ap-

Table 4. Protocol for Genetic Studies of MBD in Clinic*

(1) Identification of probands for intensive study
Positive family history; female patient; extreme response to treatment with amphetamine
(2) Single-subject comparative drug studies: clinical parameters
Amphetamine–methylphenidate equivalence
Relative potency of D- and L-amphetamine
Correlation with excitatory response to phenobarbital
(3) Neurophysiologic studies
Base-line patterns and drug-induced changes of auditory- or visual-evoked potentials
(4) Drug metabolism studies
Determination of blood levels as function of effects
Assessment of elimination rate and pattern of urinary metabolites

*University of Washington.

proach to genetic heterogeneity in the syndrome of minimal brain dysfunction. Certain patients are of special value for these investigations, for the reasons explained above. Those patients with siblings or other close relatives affected with what appears to be MBD signify families in which more than one affected individual can be tested; in such individuals similar etiologic mechanisms are likely to be at play. Biochemical and neurophysiologic results obtained for two affected members of the same family are more likely to reflect the same psychopathologic mechanism than comparable studies of two unrelated patients. Because of the sex ratio for MBD, affected girls are valuable index cases to investigate the expectations of a polygenic model. Such a model postulates a higher threshold in girls before symptoms appear; hence, a greater biologic or inherited predisposition. And for the pharmacogenetic analyses, those individuals having strikingly good or clearly negligible responses to the drug are appropriately contrasting proband groups. Because of the variability in drug responses and the extreme difficulty of matching groups of patients, single-subject drug therapy protocols have been used.[57] Teacher, parent, and physician ratings of specific undesirable and desirable behaviors provide clinical parameters of responsiveness. Both amphetamines and methylphenidate have a rapid onset of action, and 70% of a day's dose of amphetamine is normally excreted within 24 hr;[19] thus, a trial period in which two doses of drug and placebo are alternated randomly day-by-day for a mo and behaviors are scored blindly has proved a practical screen for the likely effectiveness of stimulant therapy in the individual patient.[57] The same randomized, double-blind, single-subject protocol can now be used to evaluate the equivalence of amphetamine and methylphenidate in a given individual, the relative potency of D- and L-amphetamine, and the correlation of responsiveness to stimulants with excitation by phenobarbital. These pharmacologic responses are considered by many to be the hallmarks of the clinical disorder; they are also potentially powerful means of sorting heterogeneity of causes of the syndrome.

In any behavioral genetics study, it is desirable to examine parameters at each level of expression, including clinical, neurophysiologic, and biochemical tests. At the neurophysiologic level, the use of routine EEGs has proved relatively uninformative. However, much more is expected from evoked potential studies. For example, Conners[13] reported visual-evoked potential responses in patients with learning disorders; the most striking changes occurred in a patient and his relatives who had familial dyslexia. In another study, intravenous amphetamine or methylphenidate suppressed photic driving responses in 6 of 7 hyperkinetic youngsters who had such abnormal visual-evoked responses before administration of the drug.[50] Satterfield and his colleagues[46] have reported that among a group of 31 hyperkinetic boys, the 6 best responders to methylphenidate could be distinguished from the 5 worst responders by several physiologic measures.[47] The good responders had higher mean amplitude and greater range of amplitude in the resting EEG, more movement artefacts (clinically more hyperkinetic), lower mean skin conductance, and larger auditory-evoked cortical responses. Some of the findings are consistent with the view that the nervous system is "immature" in children with MBD at a given age.[47] Studies of auditory-evoked potentials also are being carried out in our group in patients with MBD and in relatives of patients.[61]

Yet another neurophysiologic measure that has been applied to hyperactive children is electronic pupillography. Knopp et al.[29] measured the extent of pupillary contraction before and after a 5-mg test dose of amphetamine in 22 children. The greater the deviation of the child's light-reactive pupillary contraction from the normal mean before medication and the closer it approached the mean after medication, the better the correlation with a good response to D-amphetamine. These authors subdivided the 22 pupillographic responses into 5 patterns and attempted to establish some correlations with the clinical categories of hyperkinetic, overanxious, and unsocialized aggressive behavior proposed by Fish.[21]

Comparison of the effect of the potency of D and L amphetamines on clinical and neurophysiologic responses may provide clues to underlying pathophysiologic mechanisms. Amphetamines affect biogenic amine metabolism, primarily through inhibition of the neuronal reuptake mechanism. In vitro studies of isolated synaptosomes from dopamine-rich and from norepinephrine-rich regions of rat brain[55] have shown that D-amphetamine and L-amphetamine are nearly equipotent in the action on dopamine (DA) reuptake (DA lacks an optically active carbon), whereas D-amphetamine is ten times more potent than its L-stereoisomer on norepinephrine (NE) reuptake (both NE and amphetamine have an asymmetric, optically active carbon). In vivo, a locomotor activity thought to be mediated by NE in rats is enhanced by a ratio of 10:1 by D- and L-amphetamine, whereas a stereotyped gnawing behavior thought to be mediated by DA is elicited at a 1:1 to 2:1 ratio.[55] Finally, in humans, D- and L-amphetamine appear to be equipotent in inducing amphetamine psychosis, many features of which resemble schizophrenic syndromes,[1] and dopaminergic mechanisms have been postulated in schizophrenia to account for the configurational similarity to dopamine of the functional groups of chlorpromazine and other antipsychotic agents.[26]

Bradley's conclusion[6] that Dexedrine was twice as potent as Benzedrine suggests that the L-isomer is negligibly active. However, Bradley noted that the D,L-mixture was better than Dexedrine alone in some children, raising the possibility of individual differences in response, such that L-amphetamine had an independent action or acted synergistically with the D-amphetamine. Arnold et al.[3] recently carried out a double-blind cross-over comparison of D- and L-amphetamine in 11 hyperactive children, finding that the D-isomer was only slightly more effective than L-amphetamine. These data were reanalyzed in light of Fish's subclassification[21] of children with MBD; L-amphetamine seemed equally as effective as D-amphetamine in calming aggressive children, but much less effective in reducing anxiety or hyperactivity.[2] Thus, Arnold and Wender very tentatively suggest that L-amphetamine may be useful for "unsocialized aggressive" youngsters, given its lesser anorexigenic action.[2]

Two other opportunistic observations may reinforce the notion that the response to amphetamines in these children is primarily mediated through dopaminergic mechanisms. Corson et al.[15] have a model of MBD in hyperkinetic untrainable dogs. Most of their studies (personal communication) have been carried out with a single vicious cocker spaniel-beagle in a Pavlovian conditioning apparatus. The isomers of amphetamine were equally effective in suppressing aggressive behavior in this dog, while three or four times as much L-amphetamine was required in this dog and three other hyperkinetic dogs to eliminate hyperactivity (or to induce anorexia). It is not clear whether such differences reflect differential potency in central nervous system sites or different rates of metabolism of the two isomers, but the preferential action on aggressive behavior is consistent with the interpretation of the results with the children. Snyder and Meyerhoff,[54] in an excellent summary of the actions of amphetamines in the nervous system, described the responses to D- and L-amphetamine of an 8 yr-old girl, who had both MBD and the classical tic of Gilles de la Tourette's disease. D- and L-amphetamine were roughly equivalent in improving the symptoms of MBD, but only the D-isomer had any effect on the tic. As noted above, the patterns of response to D- and L-amphetamine may vary with individual patients, so additional careful clinical and pharmacologic observations will be necessary to infer the sites of action in the nervous system.

Two major explanations may account for differences in effectiveness of stimulant drugs in different children with MBD. The first has been discussed extensively already, namely, that the patients are clinically abnormal for different reasons and that certain pathogenetic mechanisms are affected by amphetamine and others are not. The second type of explanation relates to the difficult question of appropriate dosage. It is possible that individuals differ in the rate of metabolism (elimination) of the drug, so that a given dose achieves widely varying blood levels in different patients. Genetic control of the rate of metabolism of a great many drugs has been demonstrated.[39] No data are available on individual differences or even therapeutically effective blood concentrations of amphetamine, although methods for determination of amphetamine concentrations in plasma and urine are well established.[4] Patients should not be pushed to astronomical doses of drugs unless such monitoring of circulating concentrations is carried out, and unless toxicity at extremely high concentrations has been shown to be minimal.

Amphetamines are metabolized in man primarily by deamination and conjugation, but the major part of an amphetamine dose is excreted unchanged in the urine, with the amount dependent on the pH of the urine.[17] Use of radioactively labeled tracer doses of amphetamine permits determination of the pattern of metabolites excreted. Very little has been learned about the metabolism of methylphenidate, although the drug has been in use for 12 yr. Thus, amphetamine appears to be the drug of choice for correlating drug metabolism patterns with dosage and clinical responsiveness. One such study of 17 hyperkinetic children showed considerable variation in the urinary excretion of unchanged D-amphetamine, collected over 7 or 24 hr.[30] Urinary pH and urine volume contributed to the variability, but did not account for all the differences observed. Metabolites of amphetamine were not assayed. "Organic" hyperkinetic children appeared to respond better to D-amphetamine, tolerate higher doses, and excrete the drug more rapidly in the urine than did the "nonorganic" subgroup of cases. The significance of such results is not clear.

A final remark might be made with regard to the side effects and abuse potential of these drugs. Amphetamines seem not to induce tolerance in children with MBD; it is still not known whether this is a feature of childhood or of the disorders treated. Also, it is not known whether children and their families accustomed to taking behavior-modifying pharmacologic agents will be more or less likely to engage in drug experimentation later. Methylphenidate also has considerable abuse potential in adults and can induce lethal pulmonary granulomas if the suspended oral medication (containing talc as filler) is injected intravenously by addicts. Illicit traffic in Ritalin has increased among narcotic addicts for two reasons. Those on Methadone appreciate the "up" effect of Ritalin. Those on heroin can prolong the duration of action of a given dose of heroin by concomitantly taking Ritalin, because Ritalin inhibits certain drug-metabolizing enzymes in the liver.[18] Abuse of Ritalin appears to be greater in the northwest than elsewhere, but most cases probably have been unrecognized or ignored. In Chicago's Cook County prison, Ritalin is called "West Coast" by the heroin addicts, and in California it is called "Seattle."

Safer et al.[45] have introduced a disquieting issue with the report that the growth in weight and height of a small group of hyperactive children appeared to be suppressed while on amphetamine or high doses of methylphenidate. In a few children taken off drugs during the summer months, a "rebound" increase in rate of weight gain was noted. Probably these findings reflect the appetite-suppressant action of the drugs, though other mechanisms cannot be excluded. Much more extensive data will be required to evaluate this claim in relation to drug effect on the hyperactive behavior, the dosage levels, food intake, placebo effects, age, initial weight and height, and other parameters.

SUMMARY

Minimal brain dysfunction, like other complex behavioral phenotypes, is probably highly heterogeneous, with important predisposing genetic determinants in at least some cases. Additional epidemiologic studies are needed to evaluate the frequencies of MBD in general population groups and among the relatives of affected children, including twins and adopted children. Intensive clinical, psychologic, neurophysiologic, and pharmacogenetic studies of the families of selected patients may uncover specific causes of MBD, as with mental retardation syndromes. Heterogeneity of response to stimulant drugs must be sorted, so that responsive individuals can receive effective dosage, and so that unresponsive individuals can be recognized and given other therapy. Careful evaluation of the natural history of specific syndromes of MBD and of the long-term effects of stimulant drugs may provide a sounder framework for testing and treating these children.

ACKNOWLEDGMENT

I am indebted to Drs. L. E. Arnold, S. A. Corson, J. R. Morrison, M. A. Stewart, J. H. Satterfield, D. P. Cantwell, C. K. Conners, S. H. Snyder, and my colleagues B. Weber and S. Sulzbacher for making available results of studies not yet published.

REFERENCES

1. Angrist, B. M., Shopsin, B., and Gershon, S.: The comparative psychotomimetic effects of stereoisomers of amphetamine. Nature (London) 234:152, 1971.

2. Arnold, L. E., and Wender, P. H.: Levo-amphetamine's changing place in the treatment of children with behavior disorders. Pediatrics, in press.

3. —, Wender, P., McCloskey, K., and Snyder, S.: Levo-amphetamine and dextro-amphetamine: Comparative efficacy in the hyperkinetic syndrome. Arch. Gen. Psychiatry, in press.

4. Axelrod, J.: Studies on sympathomimetic amines. II. The biotransformation and physiological disposition of D-amphetamine, D-p-hydroxy-amphetamine and D-methamphetamine. J. Pharmacol. Exp. Ther. 110:315, 1954.

5. Bradley, C.: The behavior of children receiving benzedrine. Am. J. Psychiatry 94:577, 1937.

6. —: Benzedrine and Dexedrine in the treatment of children's behavior disorders. Pediatrics 5:24, 1950.

7. Cantwell, D. P.: Psychiatric illness in families of hyperactive children. Arch. Gen. Psychiatry 27:414, 1972.

8. Carter, C. O.: The inheritance of common congenital malformations. Prog. Med. Genet. 3:59, 1965.

9. Conners, C. K.: The syndrome of minimal brain dysfunction: Psychological aspects. Pediatr. Clin. North Am. 14:749, 1967.

10. —: Psychopharmacologic treatment of children. In DiMascio, A. and Shader, R. (Eds.): Clinical Handbook of Psychopharmacology. New York, Science House, 1970, p. 281.

11. —: Behavior modification by drugs. II. Psychological effects of stimulant drugs in children with minimal brain dysfunction. Pediatrics 49:702, 1972.

12. —: Stimulant drugs and cortical evoked

responses in learning and behavior disorders in children. *In* Smith, W. L. (Ed.): Drugs, Development, and Cerebral Function. Springfield, Ill., Thomas, 1972, p. 179.

13. —: Cortical visual evoked response in children with learning disorders. Psychophysiology 7:418, 1971.

14. —, Eisenberg, L., and Barcai, B. A.: Effect of dextro-amphetamine on children. Arch. Gen. Psychiatry 17:478, 1967.

15. Corson, S. A., Corson, E. O., Kirilcuk, V., and Arnold, L. E.: Tranquilizing effects of d-amphetamine on hyperkinetic untrainable dogs. Fed. Proc. 30(2):206, 1971.

16. Critchley, M.: The Dyslexic Child (ed. 2). Springfield, Ill., Thomas, 1970.

17. Davis, J. M., Kopin, T. J., Lemberger, L., and Axelrod, J.: Effects of urinary pH on amphetamine metabolism. Ann. N. Y. Acad. Sci. 179:493, 1971.

18. Dayton, P. G., and Perel, J. M.: Physiological and physicochemical bases of drug interactions in man. Ann. N. Y. Acad. Sci. 179:67, 1971.

19. Dring, L. G., Smith, R. L., and Williams, R. T.: The metabolic fate of amphetamine in man and other species. Biochem. J. 116:425, 1970.

20. Ehrhardt, A. A., and Money, J.: Progestin-induced hermaphroditism: IQ and psychosexual identity in a study of ten girls. J. Sex Res. 3:83, 1967.

21. Fish, B.: The "one child, one drug" myth of stimulants in hyperkinesis. Arch. Gen. Psychiatry 25:193, 1971.

22. Gershon, E. S., Dunner, D. L., and Goodwin, F. K.: Toward a biology of affective disorders. Arch. Gen. Psychiatry 25:1, 1971.

23. Goy, R. W.: Early hormonal influences on the development of sexual and sex-related behavior. *In* Schmitt, F. O. (Ed.): The Neurosciences, 2nd Study Program. New York, Rockefeller Press, 1970, p. 196.

24. Hallgren, G.: Specific dyslexia ("congenital word-blindness"). A clinical and genetic study. Acta Psychiatr. Neurol. Scand. (Suppl.) 65, 287 pp., 1950.

25. Heston, L. L.: Psychiatric disorders in foster home reared children of schizophrenic mothers. Br. J. Psychiatry 112:819, 1966.

26. Horn, A. S., and Snyder, S. H.: Chlorpromazine and dopamine: Conformational similarities that correlate with the antischizophrenic activity of phenothiazine drugs. Proc. Nat. Acad. Sci. U.S.A. 68:2325, 1971.

27. Jensen, A. R.: IQ's of identical twins reared apart. Behavior Genetics 1:133, 1970.

28. Knights, R. M., and Hinton, G. G.: The effects of methylphenidate (Ritalin) on the motor skills and behavior of children with learning problems. J. Nerv. Ment. Dis. 148:643, 1969.

29. Knopp, W., Arnold, L. E., Andras, R. L., and Smeltzer, D. J.: Electronic pupillography predicting amphetamine response in hyperkinetic children. Abstract, APA Meetings, May 1972, and personal communication (L. E. Arnold).

30. Lasagna, L., and Epstein, L. C.: The use of amphetamines in the treatment of hyperkinetic children. *In* Costa, E., and Garattini, S. (Eds.): Amphetamines and Related Compounds: Proc. Mario Negri Inst. Pharmacol. Res. New York, Raven Press, 1970, p. 849.

31. Laufer, M. W., and Denhoff, E.: Hyperkinetic behavior syndrome in children. J. Pediatr. 50:463, 1957.

32. Lindsley, D. B., and Henry, C. E.: The effect of drugs on behavior and the electroencephalogram of children with behavior disorders. Psychosom. Med. 4:140, 1942.

33. Lopez, R. E.: Hyperactivity in twins. Can. Psychiatr. Assoc. J. 10:421, 1965.

34. Menkes, M. M., Rowe, J. S., and Menkes, J. H.: A 25-year follow-up study on the hyperkinetic child with minimal brain dysfunction. Pediatrics 39:393, 1967.

35. Money, J., Ehrhardt, A. A., and Masica, D. N.: Fetal feminization induced by androgen insensitivity in the testicular feminization syndrome: Effect on marriage and maternalism. Johns Hopkins Med. J. 123:105, 1968.

36. Morrison, J. R., and Stewart, M. A.: A family study of the hyperactive child syndrome. Biol. Psychiatry 3:189, 1971.

37. —, and —: Studies on the adoptive relatives of hyperactive children. Personal communication, 1972.

38. Omenn, G. S.: Genetic approaches to the syndrome of minimal brain dysfunction. Ann. N. Y. Acad. Sci., in press.

39. —, and Motulsky, A. G.: Psycho-Pharmacogenetics. *In* Kaplan, A. R. (Ed.): Human Behavior Genetics. Springfield, Ill., Thomas, in press.

40. Penrose, L.: The Biology of Mental Defect (ed. 3). New York, Grune & Stratton, 1963.

41. Pratt, R. T. C.: The Genetics of Neurological Disorders. London, Oxford University Press, 1967.

42. Roberts, J. A. F.: The genetics of mental deficiency. Eugenics Rev. 44:71, 1952.

43. Rosenthal, D.: Genetic Theory and Ab-

normal Behavior. New York, McGraw-Hill, 1970.

44. Rosenthal, D., and Kety, S. S. (Eds.): The Transmission of Schizophrenia. London, Pergamon Press, 1968.

45. Safer, D., Allen, R., and Barr, E.: Depression of growth in hyperactive children on stimulant drugs. N. Engl. J. Med. 287:217, 1972.

46. Satterfield, J. H.: EEG issues in children with minimal brain dysfunction. Semin. Psychiatry 5:35, 1973.

47. —, Cantwell, D. P., Lesser, L. I., and Podosin, R. L.: Physiological studies of the hyperkinetic child. I. Am. J. Psychiatry 128: 1418, 1972.

48. Scarr-Salapatek, S.: Race, social class, and IQ. Science 175:1285, 1971.

49. Schuckit, M. A.: Family history and half-sibling research in alcoholism. In Seixas, F. A., Omenn, G. S., Burk, E. D., and Eggleston, S. A. (Eds.): Nature and Nurture in Alcoholism. Ann. N. Y. Acad. Sci. 197:121, 1972.

50. Shetty, T.: Photic responses in hyperkinesis of childhood. Science 174:1356, 1971.

51. Shields, J.: Monozygotic Twins Brought Up Apart and Brought Up Together. Oxford, Oxford University Press, 1962.

52. Sladen, B. K.: Inheritance of dyslexia. Bull. Orton. Soc. 20:30, 1970.

53. Slater, E., and Cowie, V.: The Genetics of Mental Disorders. London, Oxford University Press, 1971, Chap. 8.

54. Snyder, S. H., and Meyerhoff, J. L.: How amphetamine acts in minimal brain dysfunction. Ann. N. Y. Acad. Sci., in press.

55. —, Taylor, K. M., Coyle, J. T., and Meyerhoff, J. L.: The role of brain dopamine in behavioral regulation and the actions of psychotropic drugs. Am. J. Psychiatry 127:117, 1970.

56. Stewart, M. A., Thach, B. T., and Freidin, M. R.: Accidental poisoning and the hyperactive child syndrome. Dis. Nerv. Syst. 31:403, 1970.

57. Sulzbacher, S. I.: Diagnosis and treatment with medication of learning and behavior problems in the school-age child. Working paper #5, Child Development and Mental Retardation Center, University of Washington, 1971.

58. Vandenberg, S. G.: Contributions of twin research to psychology. Psychol. Bull. 66:327, 1966.

59. —: Hereditary factors in minimal brain damage. Ann. N. Y. Acad. Sci., in press.

60. Warren, R. J., Karduck, W. A., Bussaratid, S., Stewart, M. A., and Sly, W. S.: The hyperactive child syndrome. Normal chromosome findings. Arch. Gen. Psychiatry 24:161, 1971.

61. Weber, B., and Sulzbacher, S. I.: Unpublished observations, 1972.

62. Weiss, G., Minde, K., Werry, J. S., Douglas, V., and Nemeth, E.: Studies on the hyperactive child. VIII. Five-year follow-up. Arch. Gen. Psychiatry 24:409, 1971.

63. Wender, P. H.: Minimal Brain Dysfunction in Children. New York, Wiley-Interscience, 1971.

64. Wilson, R. S.: Twins: Early mental development. Science 175:914, 1972.

65. Winokur, G., Clayton, P. J., and Reich, T.: Manic Depressive Illness. St. Louis, Mosby, 1969.

66. Winsberg, B. G., Bialer, I., Kupietz, S., and Tobias, J.: Effects of imipramine and dextroamphetamine on behavior of neuropsychiatrically impaired children. Am. J. Psychiatry 128:1425, 1972.

Studies of Monkeys Asphyxiated at Birth: Implications for Minimal Cerebral Dysfunction

Jeri A. Sechzer, Ph.D., Maria D. Faro, Ph.D., and William F. Windle, Ph.D.

The specific neuropathology of asphyxia neonatorum is reviewed. Brain damage is demonstrable only after 7 min of asphyxia. Although the brains of monkeys asphyxiated beyond this time are considerably damaged, neurologic symptoms are transient. Developmental studies in infant monkeys, asphyxiated for 15 min, reveal the survival and normal functioning of adaptive behaviors, although they are significantly delayed in appearance. In contrast, acquired behaviors like memory and learning are severely impaired. Finally, we have compared these deficits with those observed in children with minimal cerebral dysfunction and find many striking similarities.

WELL-DOCUMENTED STUDIES have associated complications of pregnancy and birth with the appearance of the minimal cerebral dysfunction (MCD) syndrome.[18,25,38] These associations, however, lack the positive evidence that could come from appropriate animal experiments, and the fact that no animal model yet exists for minimal cerebral dysfunction is a tremendous drawback to understanding its etiology. In lieu of this, psychologic, physiologic, and more recently, neurochemical theories have been offered in an attempt to explain the constellation of symptoms presented by children with this disorder. Even though there is much literature on the physiology of the fetus and on changes that take place during the transition to early life,[6,43] it is surprising that none of these models speculate in any great detail about events that may have occurred during intrauterine life or at birth to dispose the child to this disorder. Therefore, we cannot assume with confidence that the child with MCD has not become afflicted as a result of mishaps suffered during the perinatal period.

Because MCD appears to be present from birth (excluding known postnatal events such as trauma and disease), we cannot help but feel that it will be almost impossible to determine the pathology and etiology of this condition without close scrutiny of the effects that difficulties during parturition have on the central nervous system, development, and behavior. Since one cannot experiment with the human fetus, this information will have to be derived from animal experiments in which physiologic

---

The studies included in this report were conducted at the Institute of Rehabilitation Medicine, New York University Medical Center, New York, N.Y.

Experiments were supported by National Institute of Child Health and Human Development Grant 5PO1-HD-03417, and NIH Animal Resource Branch (Division of Research Sources) Grant 5P06 RR00506, both to New York University; also supported by National Institute of Neurological Diseases and Stroke Grant 07387, and National Eye Institute Grant 00639 to Dr. Sechzer; and by the National Association for Retarded Children. Preparation of the manuscript was supported by National Science Foundation Grant GB-33469 to Dr. Sechzer, and by a grant to Dr. Faro from an anonymous foundation.

Reprint requests should be addressed to Jeri A. Sechzer, Ph.D., Edward W. Bourne Behavioral Research Laboratory, The New York Hospital-Cornell Medical Center, 21 Bloomingdale Road, White Plains, N.Y. 10605.

manipulations are made during the perinatal period. The most pertinent experiments are those that evaluate the role of asphyxia neonatorum in brain damage.

During our association at the New York University Medical Center in the Department of Rehabilitation Medicine, we were able to conduct experiments with rhesus monkeys on which asphyxial techniques were imposed at birth. It is with the implications of the effects of asphyxia neonatorum that this paper is concerned.

ASPHYXIA NEONATORUM

Asphyxia is "a condition in which there is anoxia and increased carbon dioxide tension in the blood and tissues." Asphyxia neonatorum refers to the effects of these circumstances in which the newborn is not breathing but is still alive. The lack of oxygen (anoxia) brings about respiratory acidosis, then metabolic acidosis in which the outcome can be fatal. Resuscitation and reversal of the acidosis alleviates this condition but does not always reverse the effects of asphyxia on the central nervous system. The physiologic and biochemical changes during asphyxia neonatorum have been described in detail elsewhere.[6]

Almost 30 yr ago, Windle and associates completed basic experiments with guinea pigs demonstrating a relation between structural changes of neonatal asphyxia and neurologic and learning deficits in the offspring.[2,44-46] In 1956, the work was extended to the rhesus monkey, and in 1959 the effects of asphyxia neonatorum in this species were reported for the first time.[26]

The rhesus monkey (*Macaca mulatta*) now occupies a favored position for investigations of physiology in the perinatal period. Physiologic processes are similar in both monkeys and humans; relations between fetus and mother are quite comparable. Female macaques, like women, have menstrual cycles of about 28-30 days. Placentation is similar but not identical. Maternal and fetal blood exchange through the placenta via umbilical vessels is like that of human beings. Although gestation is shorter in the monkey, 165 ± 10 days, the offspring is a little more advanced at birth than the human infant.

Of great importance are the many similarities between the fetal monkey brain and the fetal human brain, so that the neuropathology of asphyxia neonatorum is best illustrated in this nonhuman primate species.

Ranck and Windle[26] induced asphyxia by preventing the infant monkey from breathing air at the time of delivery. This technique is carried out in the fetal monkey near the end of gestation. During Cesarean section, performed with local anesthetic, the placenta is separated, the fetus and its surrounding membranes removed, and the fetal membranes kept intact until the stage of secondary apnea is reached. At this point, the membranes are opened and the fetus is delivered. Resuscitation is started by artificial ventilation of the lungs.

Duration of asphyxia has ranged from 4-21 min. Control monkeys are either delivered by Cesarean section or are born spontaneously, but they are not asphyxiated. Both experimental and control monkeys are immediately separated from their mothers. Although the infant monkeys are reared in separate cages and are never returned to their mothers, they are constantly exposed to their peers and to humans.

In the course of 15 yr of experimentation, the neuropathology and neurologic deficits of asphyxia neonatorum have been described[8,9,17,26,40-42] and confirmed by others in the monkey[22] and in the human.[5] The results of these studies show that only after 7 min of asphyxia was permanent structural brain damage consistently demonstrable.[26,39,40] More marked effects were encountered in monkeys that had been asphyxiated at birth for 8-12 min, and the more extensive damage appears in severe asphyxia of 12-17 min or longer.

Neuropathology and Neurologic Deficits

Asphyxia of 0-7 Min: Monkey fetuses can withstand nearly 7 min of asphyxia during birth without any significant signs of brain damage or neurologic deficit. These animals require no resuscitation, because they do not cease to make respiratory efforts and, therefore, do not reach the stage of secondary apnea and are not completely asphyxiated.

Asphyxia of 8-11½ Min: In all cases examined, permanent brain damage was evident when the asphyxia lasted 8-11½ min. Bilateral and symmetrical lesions were produced, sharply circumscribed by unaffected tissue. No hemorrhages were evident. The primary lesions have been localized in specific nuclei, notably those of afferent systems, except visual and olfactory. These lesions involved centers of the brain stem and diencephalon concerned with sensory input. The most vulnerable nuclei were the inferior colliculus, the ventrolateral thalamus, the sensory trigeminal, and the medial cuneate.

Surprisingly, the monkeys asphyxiated for this period of time (8-11½ min) showed only transient neurologic signs. They had trouble righting themselves and their movements were uncoordinated. Because they could not suck, they had to be hand-fed. These symptoms disappeared, often within days. It became difficult to distinguish these monkeys from nonasphyxiated control monkeys, even though their brains were structurally damaged.[8,9] They seemed to be less reactive than the controls, and some of them lacked the typical monkey emotional outbursts.[28]

Asphyxia of 12-17 Min: A more marked effect was found in infant monkeys that had been asphyxiated for this length of time. Again, the consistent pattern of bilaterally symmetrical focal lesions was found. The basic lesions of the thalamus (Fig. 1), inferior colliculi (Fig. 2), and other brain stem nuclei were more extensive and severe. Other auditory relay nuclei, including those of the lateral lemniscus and medial geniculate body, were damaged by the severity of the asphyxia. In addition to the ventrolateral group of thalamic nuclei, the medial thalamic nuclear group were also affected. Vestibular nuclei showed degeneration, and with very long duration of asphyxia the vermis and cerebellar nuclei were damaged.

All these monkeys exhibited functional deficits that persisted for some time. Righting, swallowing, sucking, and coordination were most deficient in the more severely asphyxiated animals (Fig. 3). They had poor manual dexterity[28] and showed loss of opposable thumb facility, a pattern best developed in animals of arboreal genera, to which the Macaque belongs.[19] Climbing ability was also lost in the most severely asphyxiated group.

In the course of time, the functional deficits lessened, and the animals actually seemed to compensate very well for their losses. Dexterity and coordination improved, although climbing and thumb facility were permanently lost. Casual inspection, however, revealed little or nothing of an abnormal nature. Nevertheless, study of their brains revealed progressive atrophic changes. Not only were focal scars still visible, but other regions had undergone regressive changes.[8,9] A widespread depletion of nerve-cell populations had developed in regions that had not been affected by initial asphyxia-

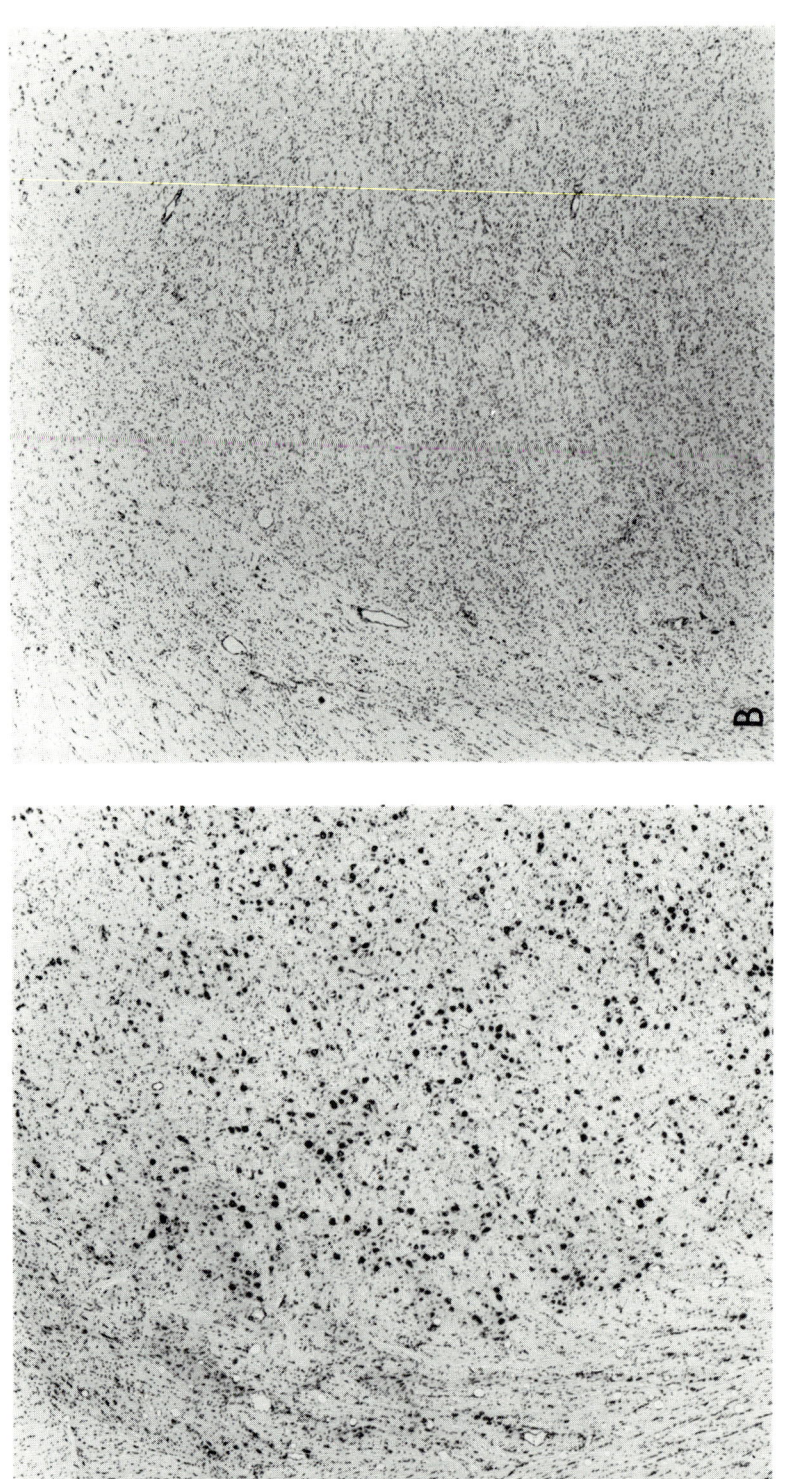

Fig. 1. Portions of the left nucleus ventralis posterior lateralis of the thalamus. (A) Nonasphyxiated monkey. (B) Monkey asphyxiated for 14.25 min, 4 yr and 9 mo ago. Comparison of the two sections shows almost total loss of nerve cells in (B), leaving what amounts to a pure population of neuroglia cells. Thionine. × 40. (Modified after Faro and Windle.[9])

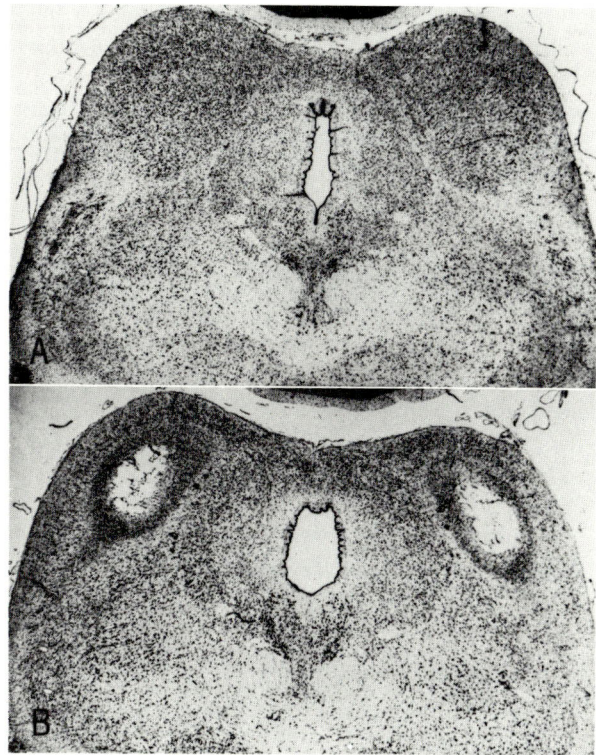

Fig. 2. Comparable sections through the mesencephalon at the level of the inferior colliculus. (A) Nonasphyxiated monkey. (B) Monkey asphyxiated 14.15 min, 4 yr and 9 mo ago with cavitation in scars of the primary lesions in the nuclei of the inferior colliculi. Comparison with (A) shows general atrophy of the colliculi with some enlargement of the aqueduct. Thionine. × 10. (Modified after Faro and Windle.[9])

tion. This was particularly noticeable in certain regions of the cerebral cortex, and it was also encountered in other parts of the thalamus, the basal ganglia, the brain stem and in the dorsal gray columns of the spinal cord. Nerve cells of these initially intact regions simply were not there. Animals that showed this type of secondary or transneuronal degeneration had been severely affected by asphyxia at birth; yet they im-

Fig. 3. (A) Normal rhesus monkey a few days after birth. This animal, typical of its species, assumes an alert, crouching stance, is curious and playful, and can feed itself easily by sucking on a bottle. At about 3 mo of age, the infant rhesus monkey will be more advanced than a human child 3 or 4 yr old. (Modified after Windle.[42]) (B) In contrast to the normal monkey, the infant rhesus monkey shown here was asphyxiated at birth for 17 min. At 8 days of age, it is still unable to use its arms and legs normally. It cannot right itself and when prodded moves with a scissors gait. This monkey required hand feeding because it could not suck. At 16 days of age, it had improved markedly; righting, sucking and swallowing reflexes appeared normal, but difficulties in locomotion persisted for some time.

proved physically while their brains continued to degenerate. It seemed that the main structural defects involved centers that are necessary to process signals from the environment and associate and integrate information. This led us to wonder whether adaptive behaviors that develop early in life are vulnerable to asphyxia, and whether acquired behaviors like memory and learning were impaired by the neuroanatomical damage so evident in the microscope.

BEHAVIOR

Development of Adaptive Behaviors

We examined the development of three kinds of adaptive behaviors in normal and neonatally asphyxiated rhesus monkeys: visual depth perception, visual placing, and independent locomotion.[35] Depth perception and placing are obviously dependent upon visual information from the environment. Independent locomotion, too, requires the utilization of external visual cues in addition to proprioceptive and kinesthetic mechanisms. The time of development of these visually dependent behaviors was of great interest to us because the visual system is spared even during severe asphyxia,[8,9,26,39] and sensory input over these pathways should proceed normally. We were evaluating integration of visual information.

Eight infant monkeys were tested. Four, delivered by Cesarean section between day 156 and day 159 of gestation, were subjected to asphyxia for 15 min and resuscitated by methods previously described.[26] The other four monkeys were nonasphyxiated controls.

Development of visual depth perception, visual placing, and locomotion was tested in all the monkeys, beginning on the first postnatal day and continuing until criterion was reached.

A modified visual cliff apparatus was used to evaluate the onset of *visual depth perception*.[35] A 76 × 76 × 61 cm masonite chamber was divided into two equal compartments (38 × 76 × 61 cm) with a 10 × 76 cm wood runway. Each compartment had a glass surface. To convey the impression that there was a shallow surface to step down onto, a red and white checkered (5 cm) panel was placed flush with the underside of the glass shelf of one compartment. To convey the impression of a deep surface, a second checkered panel was placed 41 cm below the glass shelf of the other compartment. When viewed from the runway, a sharp drop or "cliff" appeared to be present on one side of the runway, and a shallow surface on the other side of the runway.

At each trial the monkey was placed in the center of the runway and left there until it descended to the shallow or deep side or until it had remained on the runway for 2 min. A shallow or deep response was scored only when the monkey left the runway within 2 min and, with the use of all four limbs, moved its body completely onto either surface. Six random trials were given each day until the first day that 100% choice of the shallow side was reached.

Visual placing responses were tested by two methods either before or after depth perception tests. The first was to hold the monkey so that its head and limbs were unrestrained and to move it slowly toward the edge of a table until it extended its forelimbs and placed them on the table in anticipation of "landing." Three trials a day were given. The second method employed the visual cliff apparatus. Again, the monkey was supported so that its head and limbs were unrestrained; it was held in this position

10-13 cm above, and directly over, first the shallow side and then the deep side of the apparatus. The object of this test was to see when the monkey perceived the difference between the two sides and placed its limbs only on the shallow side. A positive response consisted of "placing" its limbs when it was over the shallow surface and flexing them away from the surface when it was held over the deep side. Three trials a day were given with each method until the 100% criterion was reached.

Locomotor development was evaluated daily by taking the animal out of its cage and placing it on a low table. The appropriate level of locomotion was accepted when the animal used all four limbs to crawl and could change its position independently.

The results are given in Fig. 4. Depth perception in the infant monkey normally appeared between postnatal days 3 and 5, but its onset was delayed in the asphyxiated monkeys until 12-16 days of age. Appearance of locomotion was almost parallel with that of depth perception; 3 days for the normal and 12-16 days for the asphyxiated monkeys. Visual placing responses appeared between days 3 and 7 in normal monkeys but not until days 13-17 in asphyxiated monkeys. These three- to fourfold differences between the two groups of animals are significant ($p < 0.01$).

The time of appearance of depth perception and independent locomotion in normal infant monkeys confirms that reported by others.[12,27] Even though these adaptive behaviors were delayed in the asphyxiated monkeys, there was little difference from the normal monkeys in the effectiveness with which the responses were made after they had become established.

Previous investigators have suggested[12,36] that visual depth perception is adaptive and that one of the keys to survival of a species is development of depth perception by the time locomotion becomes independent. This ability appears to be innate and does not seem to depend upon learning during early life. Evidence for this has been shown for the time of onset of visual depth perception in other animals: the chick and goat, 1 day; the rat and cat, 3-4 wk; the human infant, 6-10 mo.[12] Although the development of visual placing in the normal monkey has not been previously reported, in the cat its development usually accompanies that of depth perception.[34] We are assuming that these two behaviors also develop closely in time in the normal monkey. Because visual placing is also a type of depth perception, we are including this response as an adaptive behavior.

Although the brains of the still living monkeys will not be examined for some time,

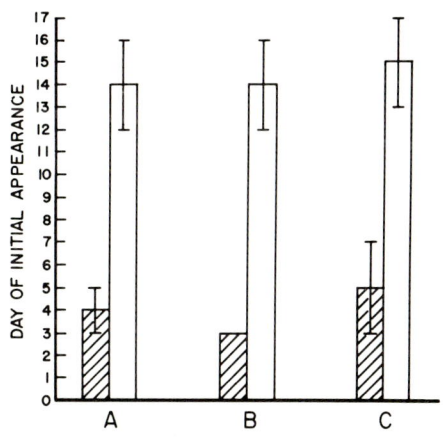

Fig. 4. The effect of birth asphyxia on development of (A) visual depth perception, (B) independent locomotion, and (C) visual placing. Hatched columns represent normal monkeys; open columns represent asphyxiated monkeys. Days are expressed as mean values; standard deviations are indicated by line segments. Differences between normal and asphyxiated monkeys in the development of all three behaviors are significant at the level of confidence $p < 0.01$ (t test). (Modified after Sechzer.[35])

we assume that they have been injured and that the pattern of damage is the same as that in other animals subjected to birth asphyxia for a comparable period of time. In spite of this damage, these adaptive behaviors were fully expressed in the asphyxiated monkeys, although significantly later than in nonasphyxiated monkeys. The survival of these adaptive or innate behaviors after asphyxia differs drastically from studies of acquired behavior to which we now turn.

Acquired Behaviors

It was important to correlate the known neuropathology and neurologic deficits of neonatal asphyxia with the level of acquisition in some of the same animals. A way to attempt this was to determine whether one or more of the essential mechanisms involved in learning were either absent or impaired. It was decided to measure memory in adult monkeys that had survived neonatal asphyxia for several years, and at the same time to obtain some measure of the animals' learning ability. A visual task was chosen to measure memory because of the marked sparing of the visual system during asphyxia. A delayed response procedure was designed to include original learning in the experiment.[32]

Delayed Response: Eight rhesus monkeys served as subjects. Four of the monkeys were asphyxiated at birth for 12-17 min and resuscitated. The other four monkeys were not asphyxiated and served as controls for the asphyxiated ones. All eight monkeys had survived in good health for 8-10 yr. (The life span of *M. mulatta* is thought to be 28-30 yr.)

Both experimental and control monkeys were trained with a visual delayed response problem. They were deprived of food for 24 hr at the onset of each daily test session. Their task was to observe, through a Plexiglass window, food being placed in one of two open wells. Both wells were then immediately covered to prevent further inspection by the monkey. At zero time and at a given number of seconds after this part of the procedure, the window was raised and the monkey permitted to choose and uncover one of the wells and take the food (Fig. 5). In order to choose consistently the correct (baited) well, the animal had to remember in which one the food had been

Fig. 5. Delayed-response apparatus suspended over cage. Door of animal's cage is open. Monkey is shown during a trial with transparent Plexiglass window raised. Position 1: pellet in food well. Position 2: monkey pushing cover aside to open well. Position 3: putting hand in well to retrieve pellet. Food wells are opaque, but for purpose of illustration are depicted as transparent. (By permission.[32])

placed. During the initial part of the experiment a learning task was imposed as one of the necessary conditions for the onset of the memory test. This was referred to as *Training with Zero Delay*. During this part of the procedure, the monkeys learned to watch the experimenter bait one of the two uncovered wells. A prearranged random series determined the right or left position for each trial.[11] As soon as both wells were covered, the window was raised and the monkey permitted to choose and uncover either the right or left well to obtain the food inside (see Fig. 5). Each animal was given 20 trials a day until its performance reached an 85% level and was maintained at this criterion for 5 consecutive days.

When each animal reached the criterion of learning, an ascending delay series was begun, first with 5-sec increments and then with 10-sec increments until 120 sec of delay was reached. The details of the procedure have been previously reported.[32] This ascending series was carried out for 10 consecutive days. Performance was averaged over the 10-day test period and recorded.

At the end of the experiment, the monkeys were not tested for 2 mo. They were retested at the end of this period for retention of the "zero delay" procedure.

Training with zero delay was started immediately after all monkeys could open the food wells, retrieve food, and correct spontaneously from one well to the other. The asphyxiated monkeys were impaired on all these habituation tasks. While control monkeys reached the 85% criterion after an average of 200 trials, asphyxiated monkeys required much longer training and reached the 85% criterion after an average of 380 trials. Although all the animals began the zero delay task at the same operational level, it was obvious that the nonasphyxiated monkeys learned faster than the asphyxiated ones.

Figure 6 compares the average performance of the control monkeys with the average performance of the asphyxiated monkeys. At zero delay, the control monkeys showed an average performance of 95% or better for 5 consecutive days prior to the onset of ascending delay. The asphyxiated monkeys performed at an average of 86%. When the delay sessions were initiated, the normal monkeys' average performance was at 95% on the 5-sec delay interval. These animals maintained a performance level of 85% and above through 50 sec of delay. Their performance began to decrease sharply after this, and at 90 sec, reached a chance level. The performance of the experimental animals, however, was quite different. When the delay test was started, the average performance

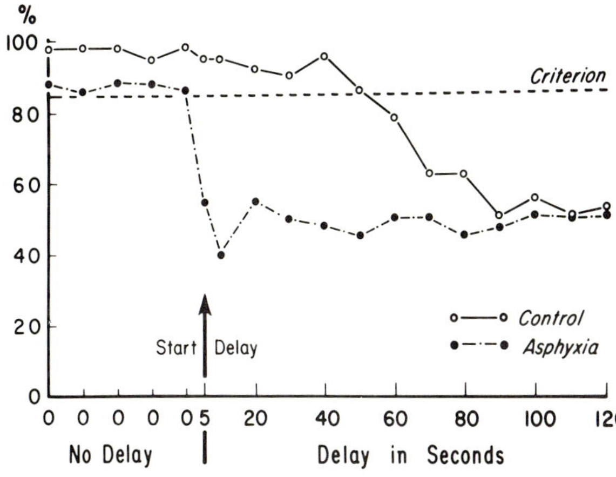

Fig. 6. Results of testing with delays of 5–120 sec. Each point on the graph gives the average performance by four control and four experimental monkeys for 10 days. Ordinate represents average percentage of correct performances for 10 days; abscissa represents delay time in sec. (By permission.[32])

of these animals fell immediately to a chance level of 55% on the 5-sec delay interval. Performance on the remainder of the ascending delay trials never improved above chance. Even on an individual level, no experimental monkey showed a performance above chance.

At the end of the 2 mo, during which there was no testing, nonasphyxiated monkeys performed with ease at criterion levels on the first test day. The asphyxiated monkeys showed immediate recognition of the problem, seemed at ease, and performed at an average of 70%. Retraining was required to bring performance with the asphyxiated monkeys back to criterion levels. Three monkeys needed 3 days of retraining, and the fourth monkey reached the criterion on the second day.

The results of this experiment clearly showed a deficit in delayed response performance of monkeys that had been subjected to asphyxia at birth, 8-10 yr previously. These impairments cannot be attributed to a visual defect. The monkeys certainly have the necessary vision to learn the task presented to them; their high level of performance on testing with zero delay in response affirms their visual ability. The visual pathways in monkeys subjected to long periods of asphyxia at birth have been found to be intact, and although the extent and severity of the brain damage of these surviving monkeys are unknown, they may be assumed to resemble the conditions in other monkeys asphyxiated for similar lengths of time.

The only interpretation that appears to account adequately for the results of this study is that these monkeys have a defect in "immediate memory." Their ability to recall immediate and transient events decays within a few seconds after the discriminating cues are removed.

Whatever loss of brain structures is associated with the memory deficits must lie in the parts of the nervous system that are damaged by asphyxiation at birth. Although the primary lesions have been localized in afferent systems (except visual), secondary or transneuronal degeneration of regions to which these nuclei project[8,9] may be involved in the memory deficit. Recent confirmation of these findings in young monkeys asphyxiated at birth has definitely associated immediate memory deficits with the primary brain damage occurring at the time of asphyxia. Hyman et al.[15] based their experiment on Sechzer's previous findings.[32] They suggested that the brain damage underlying the short-term memory deficit may be due to transneuronal degeneration. However, rhesus monkeys, asphyxiated at the time of birth and tested at 10 mo of age, were unable to perform a 5-sec delayed response task, although they did as well as normal animals with zero delay. The investigators concluded that the deficit was not of a cognitive nature, nor due to any sensory incapacity, but was truly one of short-term memory, and they support the contention that the deficit is related to primary brain damage at the time of asphyxia.

It appears from the results of these studies that short-term memory is associated with the primary brain damage of birth asphyxia. The locus of the critical region still remains to be discovered. We know, for instance, that short-term memory has been associated with the frontal lobes since Jacobsen's experiment in 1935.[16] Primary damage from asphyxia does not include the frontal lobe, and the memory deficits then must be associated with lesions in other areas. This conclusion is contrary to much of the literature on this subject,[4,10,13,20,21,24,25] which links delayed response deficits with frontal lobe lesions. Schulman,[31] however, reported severe short-term memory impairment after extensive lesions of the dorsomedial nucleus of the thalamus of adult rhesus monkeys. His study may have relevance since primary damage by birth asphyxia has been found in the dorsomedial thalamic nucleus of the medial thalamic group.[8,9]

Discrimination Learning: Studies at zero delay suggested that, although the visual system is not defective, at least for simple right-left orientation, visual learning in monkeys asphyxiated at birth may require prolonged training. To answer this question, we conducted a pattern discrimination[33] with the same monkeys that had already been tested on delayed response.[32] We used the same test paradigm with the same apparatus as before but with two changes. An opaque window was substituted for the transparent window that we used during zero and delayed response testing. It eliminated food as a visual cue and the monkey had to learn the association between a specific stimulus and the nonvisible food reward. We also covered one food well with an upright triangle and the other food well with an inverted triangle. These two stimuli were identical, differing only in orientation. On each trial, food was placed in the well covered by the stimulus designated to be correct. Each monkey was trained to select the positive stimulus, and to push it away to expose and obtain the food in the well. Correction for errors was permitted. Twenty trials a day were given to each animal until a performance of 90% or better was reached and maintained for 3 consecutive days.

The normal monkeys learned the discrimination, reaching the criterion in an average of 270 trials; the asphyxiated group did not learn the discrimination in 750 trials. Their level of performance was never higher than 65%, and this only occasionally. Most of the asphyxiated group responded with strong position preferences (right or left) after the first few training trials. Regardless of how much coaxing and regardless of how little time elapsed between trials, they still did not demonstrate any attempt to discriminate the stimuli. It was almost as if they gave up shortly after training began.

It is interesting that in a simple black-white visual discrimination conducted by Hyman et al.,[15] both asphyxiated and normal monkeys learned at the same rate. These monkeys, however, were 10 mo of age and our monkeys were 8-10 yr of age. The monkeys in Hyman's experiment were not tested on a more complex visual task, nor were our monkeys tested on a black-white discrimination. The same group found that monkeys asphyxiated at birth could perform well on signaled shock-avoidance tasks but were severely impaired on the same task when the preshock signal was eliminated.[14] These results are in many ways comparable to our findings with zero delay and with ascending delay in that the animal has difficulty in remembering for any period of time past a few seconds when the presence of the effective stimulus is removed.

The results of these studies of impaired learning by monkeys subjected to asphyxia neonatorum suggest three possibilities. First, the lack of positive reinforcement or the experience of negative reinforcement (shock) is not very effective. Second, the animal's memory, long-term as well as short-term, is severely impaired; this is suggested in our visual tasks by the lack of progress in visual learning during the session and from one day's session to the next day's session. The third possibility is that fewer nerve cells are required for adaptive behaviors than for acquired behaviors. The brain damage of asphyxia neonatorum undoubtedly reduces the number of nerve cells and, although there are sufficient numbers for the development of adaptive behaviors, there are not enough for acquisition.

Some support for this possibility comes from the work of Balázs et al.[1] and of Schapiro,[29,30] who treated newborn rat pups with thyroid hormone. Balázs killed the animals at various ages and found that $3,3',5$ triiodo-L-thyronine (T_3) affects cell for-

Table 1. Comparison of Results Shown by Children With MCD and by Monkeys Asphyxiated at Birth

Characteristics of MCD Children		Behavioral Studies With Asphyxiated Monkeys	
Behavior	Disorder	Experimental Method	Experimental Results
Motor activity	Hyperactivity	Observations of activity (1) In cage (2) During testing	*In cage:* Hyperactivity is present and is especially marked in young animals; they are in constant motion rather than showing excessive motion; adults show less activity and tend to become quieter with increasing age. *During testing:* The animals' activity levels decrease and they tend to stay in one place during the test session
Developmental milestones	?	Righting reflexes; independent locomotion; visual depth perception; visual placing	All these behaviors show at least a threefold delay in the time of appearance but are normal in efficiency
Coordination	Visuomotor incoordination; clumsiness; poor balance	Climbing in cage; locating targets; grasping objects	*Climbing ability:* Markedly impaired, and in severely asphyxiated monkeys can be lost completely; when the animals do climb there is imbalance, also seen when they are sitting or moving about in their cages; there is always improvement with time but impairment is not always completely reversible in severely asphyxiated monkeys. *Locating targets* is difficult, the monkeys misreach and require several trials for correct location. *Grasping objects* and holding them is defective; for example, some monkeys cannot get food to their mouths efficiently with their hands and resort to eating like dogs
Attention	Decreased attention span; poor coordination	Habituation to delayed response and visual discrimination tests; auditory thresholds and response to sounds; response to moving objects	*Habituation:* Takes longer in asphyxiated monkeys; they require more practice until they can watch the stimuli or food adequately, even though they appear to be very hungry. *Auditory thresholds* are elevated, and response to sound is moderate and slow[3]

Learning and memory	Deficits in memory; impairments in learning	Delayed response test; signaled and unsignaled shock-avoidance tests; visual discrimination test	*Moving objects* elicit no sudden response nor is there rapid following with head and eyes, as is demonstrated by the normal monkey *Zero delay test* involves prolonged learning *Ascending delay test* shows that the animals could not remember where food was placed at delays of 5 sec or more *Signaled shock-avoidance* learning is normal but when *unsignaled shock-avoidance* is tested, the monkeys cannot perform *Visual discrimination test* shows that asphyxiated monkeys cannot learn in twice the number of trials required by the normal monkeys
Impulse control	Decreased ability to inhibit responses	Perseveration of errors and position habits	Persistent choice of either the right or left object or side results in chance levels of performance and 50% errors; this appears to be a contributing factor in the excessive number of training trials necessary to reach the criterion of learning
Emotionality	Reactivity, increased or decreased; lowered frustration tolerance	Changes in environment; response to noise; response to strangers and objects; response to positive and negative reinforcement	*Hyporeactivity* is generally observed after changes in environment, and to noise, strangers and objects; there is little curiosity or excitability with reduced emotional outbursts; when an error is made during delayed response testing, thereby delaying positive reinforcement of food, the monkey does not hasten to correct its error and often just stares into space for short periods of time before going to the correct side, yet eats rapidly and appears hungry; with shock-avoidance tests, the monkey responds only to the experience of shock but not to the anticipation of shock. These animals are deficient in their response to positive and negative reinforcement, responding like the normal monkey only under very specific conditions

mation, resulting in a 30%–40% reduction in the number of cells formed after birth. Schapiro did not look at the histology but tested the animals during early life and again as adults. He found that such treatment accelerates behavioral and neurophysiologic development of the brain and adaptive behaviors but impairs learning of older animals. These two series of experiments suggest that fewer nerve cells are needed for the elicitation and performance of early developmental behaviors, but that later, when more complex tasks are required of the animal, the additional nerve cells needed for their performance are not available.

IMPLICATIONS FOR MINIMAL CEREBRAL DYSFUNCTION

It is evident that asphyxia neonatorum leaves its mark on the structure of the brain. The correlation of the neuropathology of asphyxia has been demonstrated in monkeys by neurologic aberrations, by delays in development of adaptive behaviors, and by severe impairments in acquired behaviors.

What are the implications of these studies? Can they tell us anything about MCD in children? We have compared characteristics found in children with MCD with deficits in monkeys asphyxiated at birth. In children, this disorder is manifested by quantitative differences in the following behaviors: motor activity, coordination, attention span, learning, impulse control, and interpersonal relations and emotionality. Thus, hyperactivity, visuomotor incoordination, decreased attention span, impaired memory (both short- and long-term), inability to inhibit responses, hyperreactivity and sometimes hyporeactivity, and anhedonia (the decreased ability to experience pleasure or pain or the decreased ability to respond to negative or positive reinforcement) are some of the common dysfunctions presented by afflicted children.[37]

An appropriate animal model, then, would have to satisfy the following criteria: (1) symptoms should be evident, in part, from birth; (2) other symptoms should appear at comparable ages as they do in children; (3) the animals should be manageable by amphetamine or amphetamine-like drugs and respond (as so many children do) with a decrease in activity and an increase in attention, learning, and memory; and (4) the opportunity to analyze the brains of the animals for pathologic changes utilizing classical histologic techniques; histofluorescent methods to identify and differentiate monoamine pathways (norepinephrine, dopamine, and serotonin); and biochemical assays to quantify monoamine levels in the brain.

That the effects of neonatal asphyxia mimic many of the symptoms shown by children with MCD is shown in Table 1. We have compared the results of our studies of monkeys asphyxiated at birth with some of the disorders of children with this syndrome. The two left-hand columns list the clinical characteristics of children with MCD. The third column lists the experimental procedures by which an analogous deficit might be elicited in the monkey. The fourth column gives the actual experimental results. Many of them correlate well with clinical features, some with statistical significance.

None of the monkeys have been tested with amphetamine or amphetamine-like drugs. We have no information on their endocrine levels or amine activity. Developmental milestones are delayed significantly in the asphyxiated monkeys, but there are no definitive data available on the time of the appearance of these adaptive behaviors in children with MCD (see Table 1). Although the brains of the asphyxiated monkeys continue to degenerate, there has not been an opportunity to assess the effects of this process on their life span, nor do we have this information for human beings. It is also important to note that, although the neuropathology and neurologic deficits have been demonstrated for monkeys asphyxiated up to 17 min at birth, developmental and behavioral deficits have been demonstrated only in monkeys asphyxiated for 12-17 min. We do not know whether behavioral studies of monkeys asphyxiated for short periods (with no observable neurologic signs) would show even greater similarity to children with MCD than the present studies do.

The fact that the human brain is less mature at birth than that of the monkey may render it more resistant to brain damage. Therefore, the MCD child would not be as neurologically impaired as the monkey after asphyxia for comparable periods.

If the monkey suffering asphyxia neonatorum could serve in part as an animal model, we could then begin to compare some of the deficits with those shown by affected children and approach some understanding of the mechanisms underlying this disorder.

REFERENCES

1. Baláazs, R., Kovacs, S., Cocks, W. A., Johnson, J. L., and Eayrs, J. T.: Effect of thyroid hormone on the biochemical maturation of rat brain: Postnatal cell formation. Brain Res. 25:555, 1971.
2. Becker, R. F., and Donnell, W.: Learning behavior in guinea pigs subjected to asphyxia at birth. J. Comp. Physiol. Psychol. 45:153, 1952.
3. Berman, D., Karalitzky, A. R., and Berman, A. J.: Auditory thresholds in monkeys asphyxiated at birth. Exp. Neurol. 31:140, 1971.
4. Blum, J. S., Chow, K. L., and Blum, R. A.: Delayed response performance of monkeys with frontal removals after excitant and sedative drugs. J. Neurophysiol. 14:197, 1951.
5. Brierly, J. B. The influence of brain swelling, age, and hypotension upon the pattern of cerebral damage in hypoxia. In Lüthy, F., and Bischoff, A. (Eds.): Proceedings of the Fifth International Congress of Neuropathology. Amsterdam, Excerpta Medica, 1966, p. 21.
6. Dawes, G. S.: Foetal and Neonatal Physiology. Chicago, Year Book, 1968.
7. Eayrs, J. T.: Developmental relationships between brain and thyroid. In Michael, R. P. (Ed.): Endocrinology and Human Behavior, London, Oxford University Press, 1968, p. 239.
8. Faro, M. D., and Windle, W. F.: Progressive degenerative changes in brains of monkeys surviving neonatal asphyxia. In James, L. S., Meyers, R. E., and Guall, G. E. (Eds.): Brain Damage in the Fetus and Newborn from Hypoxia or Asphyxia. Columbus, Ohio, Ross Laboratories, 1967, p. 24.
9. —, and —: Transneuronal degeneration in brains of monkeys asphyxiated at birth. Exp. Neurol. 24:38, 1969.
10. Finan, J. L.: Delayed response with predelay reinforcement in monkeys after removal of the frontal lobes. Am. J. Psychol. 55:202, 1942.
11. Gellerman, L. W.: Chance orders of alternating stimuli on visual discrimination experiments. J. Genet. Psychol. 42:206, 1933.
12. Gibson, E. J., and Walk, R. D.: Sci. Am. 202 (4):64, 1960.
13. Harlow, H. F., Davis, R. T., Settlage, P. H., and Meyers, D. R.: Analysis of frontal and posterior association syndromes in brain-damaged monkeys. J. Comp. Physiol. Psychol. 45:419, 1952.
14. Hyman, A., Berman, D., and Berman, A. J.: Deficits in unsignaled avoidance behavior in rhesus monkeys asphyxiated at birth. Exp. Neurol. 30:362, 1971.
15. —, Parker, B., Berman, D., and Berman, A. J.: Delayed response deficits in neonatally asphyxiated monkeys. Exp. Neurol. 28:420, 1970.
16. Jacobsen, C. F.: Functions of frontal association area in primates. Arch. Neurol. Psychiatry 33:558, 1935.
17. Jacobson, H. N. and Windle, W. F.: Responses of foetal and newborn monkeys to asphyxiation. J. Physiol. 153:447, 1960.
18. Knobloch, H., and Pasamanick, B.: Prospective studies on the epidemiology of reproductive causality: Methods, findings and some implications. Presented at the Merrill-Palmer Institute Conference on Research and Teaching of Infant Development, Feb. 11, 1965. Unpublished.
19. LeGros Clark, W. E.: The Antecedents of Man. Chicago, Quadrangle Books, 1960, p. 206.
20. Malmo, R. B.: Interference factors in

delayed response in monkeys after removal of frontal lobes. J. Neurophysiol. 5:295, 1942.

21. Meyer, D. R., Harlow, H. F., and Settlage, P. H.: A survey of delayed response performance by normal and brain damaged monkeys, J. Comp. Physiol. Psychol. 44:17, 1951.

22. Meyers, R. E.: Patterns of perinatal brain damage in the monkey. *In* James, L. S., Meyers, R. E., and Guall, G. E. (Eds.): Brain Damage in the Fetus and Newborn from Hypoxia or Asphyxia. Columbus, Ohio, Ross Laboratories, 1967.

23. Miles, R. C., and Bloomquist, A. J.: Frontal lesions and behavioral deficits in monkeys. J. Neurophysiol. 23:471, 1960.

24. Mishkin, M. Rosvald, H. E. and Pribram, K. H.: Effects of nembutal in baboons with frontal lesions. J. Neurophysiol. 16:155, 1953.

25. Montagu, A.: Prenatal Influences. Springfield, Ill., Thomas, 1962.

26. Ranck, J. R., and Windle, W. F.: Brain damage in the monkey *Macaca mulatta*, by asphyxia neonatorum. Exp. Neurol. 1:130, 1959.

27. Rosenblum, L. A., and Cross, H. A.: Performance of neonatal monkeys in the visual cliff situation. Am. J. Psychol. 76:318, 1963.

28. Saxon, S. V., and Ponce, C. G.: Behavioral defects in monkeys asphyxiated during birth. Exp. Neurol. 4:460, 1961.

29. Schapiro, S.: Effects of thyroxine on maturation and development of the infant rat. Endocrinology 78:527, 1966.

30. —: Influence of hormones and environmental stimulation on brain development. Presented at the International Society of Psychoneuroendocrinology Conference on the Influence of Hormones on the Nervous System, New York, 1970. Basel, Karger, 1971.

31. Schulman, S.: Impaired delayed response from thalamic lesion. Arch. Neurol. 11:477, 1964.

32. Sechzer, J. A.: Memory deficit in monkeys brain damaged by asphyxia neonatorum. Exp. Neurol. 24:497, 1969.

33. —: Impairment of learning in adult rhesus monkeys surviving neonatal asphyxia. Unpublished results.

34. —: Development of adaptive behavior in normal and split-brain cats. Unpublished results.

35. —, Faro, M. D., Barker, J. N., Barsky, D., Gotierrez, S., and Windle, W. F.: Developmental behaviors: Delayed appearance in monkeys asphyxiated at birth. Science 171:1173, 1971.

36. Walk, R. D., and Gibson, E. J.: A comparative and analytical study of visual depth perception. Psychol. Monogr. 75:519, 1961.

37. Wender, P. H.: Minimal Brain Dysfunction in Children. New York, Wiley-Interscience, 1971.

38. Werry, J. S.: Studies on the hyperactive child: An empirical analysis of the minimal brain dysfunction syndrome. Arch. Gen. Psychiatry 19:9, 1968.

39. Windle, W. F.: Structural and functional alterations in the brain following neonatal asphyxia. Psychosom. Med. 6:155, 1944.

40. —: Neuropathology of certain forms of mental retardation. Science 140:1186, 1963.

41. —: Brain damage at birth. Functional and structural modifications with time. JAMA 206:1967, 1968.

42. —: Brain damage by asphyxia at birth. Sci. Am. 221 (4):76, 1969.

43. —: Physiology of the Fetus: Relation to Brain Damage in the Perinatal Period. Springfield, Ill., Thomas, 1971.

44. —, and Becker, R. F.: Effects of anoxia at birth on the central nervous system of the guinea pig. Proc. Soc. Exp. Biol. Med. 51:213, 1942.

45. —, and —: Asphyxia neonatorum. Am. J. Obstet. Gynecol. 45:183, 1943.

46. —, Becker, R. F., and Weil, A.: Alteration in brain structure after asphyxiation at birth. J. Neuropathol. Exp. Neurol. 3:224, 1944.

EEG Issues in Children With Minimal Brain Dysfunction

James H. Satterfield, M.D.

An evoked cortical response study of 31 minimal brain dysfunction (MBD) children and 21 normal controls revealed that MBD children have longer latency and lower amplitude evoked cortical responses. A study of 57 MBD children showed that those with either an abnormal EEG or four or more soft signs on neurologic examination had a better response to methylphenidate treatment than did those children in whom these abnormalities were absent. These findings suggest a delayed maturation of the central nervous system in some MBD children.

THE EEG PROVIDES AT BEST a very crude measurement of brain activity. The interpretation of the EEG in children is further complicated by major changes associated with maturation.[3,10] The relationship between the EEG and other measures of neurologic dysfunction has been found to be quite low in several studies,[9,18] as has the relationship between the EEG and psychiatric diagnoses in children.[11] Most studies of minimal brain dysfunction (MBD) in children have reported an increased incidence of EEG abnormalities.[5,21,22] However, the relevance of an abnormal EEG in MBD children is not well established owing to the fact that there are so few investigations of the incidence of EEG abnormalities in blindly rated control groups.

Two well-designed studies that utilized blindly rated control groups were conducted by Caputano et al.[1] and by Hughes.[4] Caputano studied a group of children with minimal brain dysfunction, all of whom had soft neurologic signs, which made this sample a special one, since only about half of nonselected MBD children have such signs.[16,21] They reported that 8% of 106 children had marked EEG abnormalities, and 43% mild-to-moderate ones, compared to 17% of mild to moderate EEG abnormalities in a normal control group. Hughes compared 214 children who were underachievers with a like number of normal controls. The incidence of EEG abnormalities in the underachiever group was 41.2%, which was significantly higher than in the control group, which had an incidence of only 29.8% ($p < 0.007$).

Although it would seem that MBD children have significantly more EEG abnormalities than normals, the usefulness of the EEG as a diagnostic aid may be limited by the higher number of normal children (albeit with lower incidence of EEG abnormalities). As has been shown by Wender,[21] one can estimate the fraction of all children with abnormal EEGs who also have MBD. Let us take Caputano's findings of 43% EEG abnormalities in MBD children and 17% in normal children, and apply these figures to 1000 children selected at random from the general population. The general prevalence of MBD is estimated to be 5%; therefore, of these 1000 children, 50 would have MBD and 950 would not. Of these 1000 children, 17% of 950 (161 normal children) would have abnormal EEGs, and 43% of 50 (21 MBD children) would have abnormal EEGs.

Supported in part by NIMH Grant MH 17039, a grant from the Andrew Norman Foundation, a grant from the Julius R. Wolf Foundation, and a grant from Ciba Pharmaceutical Company.

Reprint requests should be addressed to James H. Satterfield, M.D., Gateways Hospital, 1891 Effie Street, Los Angeles, Calif. 90026.

Therefore, of the 182 children with abnormal EEGs, 21 (about 11%) would have MBD. This is a discouragingly small number, and if used solely as a diagnostic test would be wrong 89% of the time. Furthermore, 60% of MBD children with no signs of brain dysfunction (normal EEGs and normal neurologics) have been shown to obtain a good response to stimulant drug treatment.[16] All of this makes one indeed wonder as to the clinical relevance of the EEG in children with MBD.

We would like to report on two studies, reported in part elsewhere,[16] which suggest that EEG measures and other neurologic data have relevance for both diagnosis and response to treatment in MBD children.

EXPERIMENT I

This is a study of clinical EEGs, neurologic examinations, and responses to methylphenidate treatment in a group of 57 MBD children.

Method

Subject Selection: All MBD children were referred to Gateways Hospital's children's clinic for evaluation and treatment. To be included in this study, an MBD patient had to be (1) male; (2) between the ages of 6 and 9 yr; (3) attending school; (4) without sensory defects; (5) at or above 80 in IQ on the Wechsler Intelligence Scale for Children (WISC Full Scale); (6) off medication for a period of at least 3 mo prior to testing; (7) diagnosed independently by two child psychiatrists as having MBD; and (8) diagnosed as suffering from the MBD Child Syndrome by the criteria of Stewart et al.,[19] which require definite evidence of hyperactivity and distractibility and the presence of any 6 of the 28 symptoms found to be most characteristic of the syndrome. Normal control subjects were paid volunteers who met all of the same selective criteria except the last two.

Social Evaluation: A structured interview was obtained on all subjects, which included the following: identification (15 items); history of present illness, behavior and symptom inventory (54 items); developmental history (13 items); past medical history (9 items); and family history (25 items). A teacher rating scale was obtained on all subjects before and after treatment. The rating scale for teachers consisted of 30 items of classroom behavior arranged in a checklist form so that the teacher could check off whether each individual item of behavior was exhibited by the child: (1) not at all; (2) just a little; (3) pretty much; (4) very much. These individual ratings were given numerical scores of 0, 1, 2, and 3, respectively, and then summed to give a total rating score across all behavioral items. Thus, higher scores on the teacher's rating scale reflect more disturbed behavior. These scales have been demonstrated to have high test-retest reliability[13] and to validly differentiate placebo from methylphenidate treatment groups.[15] Lack of improvement, or deterioration, was indicated by no change or by an increase in the score following treatment.

Neurologic Evaluation: Clinical EEGs and neurologic examinations were obtained on all patients. The neurologic examination was operationally defined as abnormal if one or more of the following "soft signs" were present: (1) impairment of fine motor coordination; (2) synkinesis; (3) choreoathetosis; (4) speech disorder; (5) motor impersistence; (6) reflex asymmetry; (7) motor weakness; (8) gait disturbance.

The EEGs were obtained by the 10-20 international system of electrode placement, and with an eight-channel Grass EEG machine. Both referential and bipolar montages were used, and the EEG included a recording during wakefulness with 3-5 min of hyperventilation.

Psychiatric Evaluation: All patients were independently evaluated by two child psychiatrists utilizing a structured interview.

Evaluation of Response to Treatment: Results of methylphenidate treatment were obtained on 57 MBD children from a double-blind methylphenidate-placebo treatment study. Treatment was carried out for a 3-wk period. The dosage was adjusted upward at weekly intervals until a good clinical response was obtained, or until side effects prohibited further increase. Teacher rating scales were obtained before and immediately after 3 wk of treatment. Percentage of change in the teacher rating scale was taken as the measure of response to treatment, and was defined as the initial teacher rating minus the final rating, divided by the initial rating.

Psychological Evaluation: All subjects were administered a battery of psychologic tests, including the WISC, the Wide Range Achievement Test (WRAT), the Illinois Test of Psycholinguistic Abilities (ITPA), the Goodenough-Harris Draw-A-Person, the Bender-Gestalt, and the Lincoln Oseretsky.

Laboratory Studies: Laboratory studies included power spectral analyses of the EEG, auditory-evoked cortical responses, and skin conductance level (SCL). Results of the SCL studies of MBD children were previously reported.[14]

Results

The results of the clinical EEG and neurologic examinations are shown in Fig. 1. It can be seen that 18 of 57 MBD children had abnormal EEGs and 29 of 57 had abnormal neurologic examinations.

The 18 subjects with abnormal EEGs (both those with and without abnormal neurologic examinations) had a mean improvement of 51%, compared to a mean improvement of only 29% in the group with normal EEGs—a difference that is statistically sig-

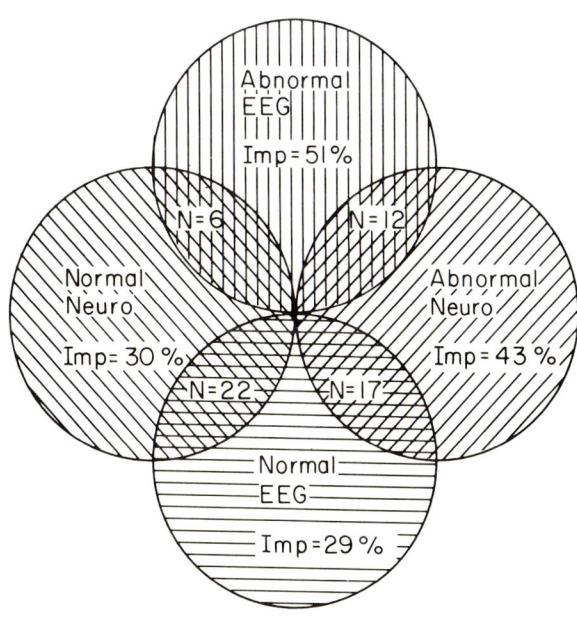

Fig. 1. Diagram showing distribution of EEG and neurologic abnormalities in 57 MBD children. Percentage of improvement in response to methylphenidate treatment is also shown.

nificant ($p < 0.01$, Mann-Whitney U Test). However, if we eliminate from that group those subjects who also had abnormal findings on neurologic examination, we are left with six subjects with abnormal EEGs but normal neurologics. When we compare this group (mean improvement of 46%) with the normal EEG group (mean improvement of 29%), the difference is no longer statistically significant. When we compare all 29 MBD children with abnormal neurologics (mean improvement of 43%) with the 28 MBD children with normal neurologics (mean improvement of 30%), we find they are significantly different ($p < 0.05$). However, when we remove from this group the 12 children who also had abnormal EEGs, we are left with 17 MBD children with only abnormal neurologics (mean improvement of 35%), and this group does not differ significantly from the normal neurologic group with its mean improvement of 30%.

On first examination it appears that the presence of either abnormality (EEG or neurologic examination) predicts a good response to treatment. However, this is more apparent than real, since the good response in both of these groups is due to the 12 subjects with both abnormalities. A better interpretation of these data is that the presence of both abnormalities predicts a good response to treatment.

Since both neurologic and EEG data were available on all subjects, each patient fell into one of four subgroups, depending upon the presence or absence of an abnormal EEG, and the presence or absence of an abnormal neurologic examination. The subgroups were as follows: (1) both EEG and neurologic abnormalities, 12 subjects; (2) an abnormal neurologic but normal EEG, 17 subjects; (3) normal on both EEG and neurologic, 22 subjects; and (4) abnormal EEG but normal neurologic, 6 subjects.

When response to methylphenidate treatment is compared in these four groups, we find that the group with normal EEG and normal neurologic had a mean improvement of 25%; the group with only an abnormal neurologic had a mean improvement of 35%; the group with only an abnormal EEG had a mean improvement of 46%; and the group with both EEG and neurologic abnormalities had a mean improvement of 55% (Fig. 2). It can be seen that there is a definite trend of increasing clinical improvement as we go from the normal-normal group to the abnormal neurologic group, to the abnormal EEG group, and to the group with both EEG and neurologic abnormalities. However, these group differences in response to treatment are statistically significant only for the group with both abnormalities. This group with both abnormal EEG and abnormal neurologic improved significantly more than did the group with only abnormal neurologic examinations ($p < 0.05$), and more than the group with both normal EEG and normal neurologic ($p < 0.001$, Mann-Whitney U Test). It is interesting to note that most of the treatment failures were in the group with both normal neurologic and EEG findings.

These EEG and neurologic findings suggested that these measures were relevant to the response of the MBD child to treatment. Thus encouraged, we decided to take a closer look at both the EEG and neurologic measures. We first re-examined the EEG records and divided the 18 patients with EEG abnormalities into two groups: those with a borderline abnormal EEG, and those with a definitely abnormal EEG. Records were considered to be borderline when excessive slow activity or sharp transients were noted, which could not be clearly differentiated from (1) movement, electrode or machine-generated artefact; or (2) physiologic patterns encountered in normal drowsiness and light sleep. A record was considered definitely abnormal when one or both of the following were present: (1) excessive slow wave (theta or delta) activity, generally associated with fair to poor organization (lack of rhythmicity) and development (re-

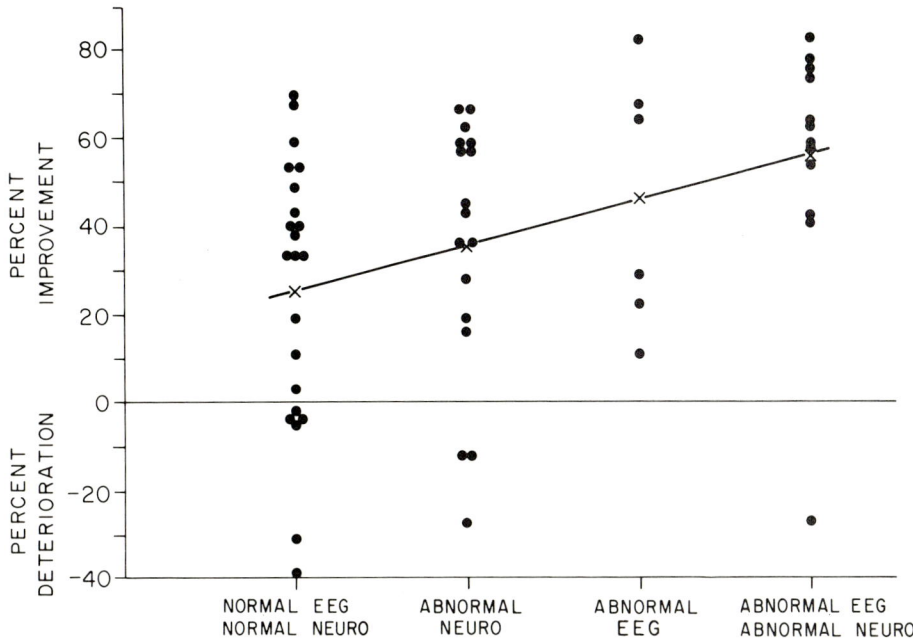

Fig. 2. Improvement in response to methylphenidate treatment shown for four major subject-groups of MBD children classified on basis of presence of abnormal EEG or neurologic examination.

duced amplitude) of the EEG; (2) frequent epileptiform (sharp or spike wave) discharges. Organization of the EEG was assessed during the patient's most relaxed state. Focal abnormalities (slow wave or epileptiform discharges) were most commonly seen in the temporal-occipital regions.

Soft signs from the neurologic examination were arbitrarily grouped into one of ten categories (Table 1). The most common soft sign category was fine motor incoordination of the hands (16 patients). The observed range of the soft sign categories was zero to five. Response to treatment was then compared in the three following groups of patients classified on the basis of the EEG data: (1) normal EEG; (2) borderline EEG; (3) abnormal EEG. Response to treatment was also compared in the following three groups of patients classified according to the number of soft sign categories present: (1) zero categories; (2) one to two categories, and (3) four to five categories.

Table 1. Number of MBD Children With Neurologic Soft Signs in Each Category

Soft Sign	Number of Cases
Upper extremity fine motor incoordination or weakness	16
Synkinesis, or motor inpersistence	13
Hyperactive or asymmetrical reflexes	11
Choreiform movements, or abnormal posturing of the hands and fingers	10
Lower extremity fine motor incoordination or weakness	9
Dysarthria or infantile speech	5
Equivocal plantar response	4
Gait or balance disorder	3
Deviant hand preference	3
Discriminative sensory loss	2

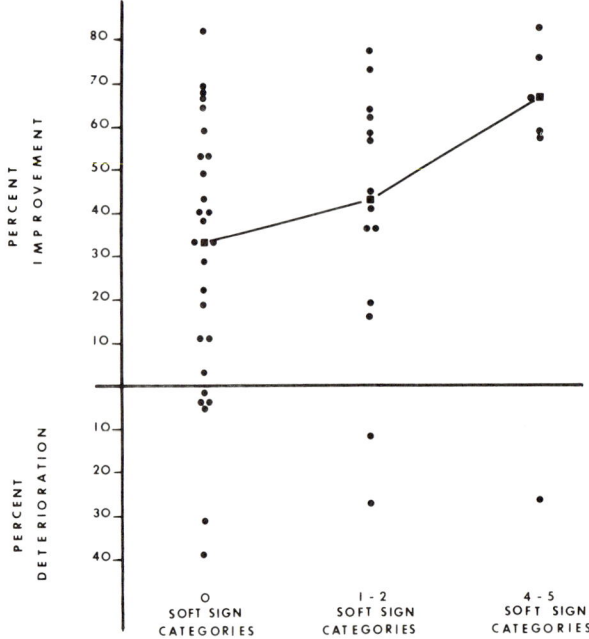

Fig. 3. Percentage of change in teacher rating scale following methylphenidate treatment in MBD children with neurologic findings in (1) zero soft sign categories, (2) one or two soft sign categories, and (3) four or five soft sign categories.

Neurologic Findings: Patients with neurologic soft signs in four to five categories obtained a better response to treatment than did those patients with fewer signs (Fig. 3). There is a trend of increasing improvement as one goes from the group with no soft signs, to the group with only one to two categories of soft signs, to the group with four to five categories of soft signs. However, the only statistically significant difference is between the group with four to five categories of soft signs and the group with no soft signs ($p < 0.01$, Mann-Whitney U Test).

Electroencephalographic Findings: Seven patients had a borderline EEG and eleven patients had a definitely abnormal EEG. No frank seizure patterns were present in any subject. Of the eleven patients with definite EEG abnormalities, four had excessive slow wave activity, three had epileptiform discharges, and four exhibited both slow wave and epileptiform activity. In this same group two patients had generalized, three focal, and six both generalized and focal EEG abnormalities.

There was a trend toward increased response to treatment from the patient group with normal EEGs to the group with borderline EEGs, to the group with abnormal EEGs (Fig. 4). The abnormal EEG group had significantly more improvement than did the borderline EEG group ($p < 0.01$), and also greater improvement than the normal EEG group ($p < 0.001$, Mann-Whitney U Test).

Since the presence of four or more soft sign categories or the presence of an abnormal EEG (each considered separately) was found to predict a good response to treatment, we investigated whether one of these measures added any predictability to the other. To examine this question patients were arbitrarily assigned to the following groups: (1) patients who had neurologic soft signs in two or less categories, and (2) patients with soft signs in three or more categories. Patients were also divided into (1) a borderline or normal EEG group, and (2) an abnormal EEG group. This classification results in four groups in which we can separate out the effect of the type of EEG and

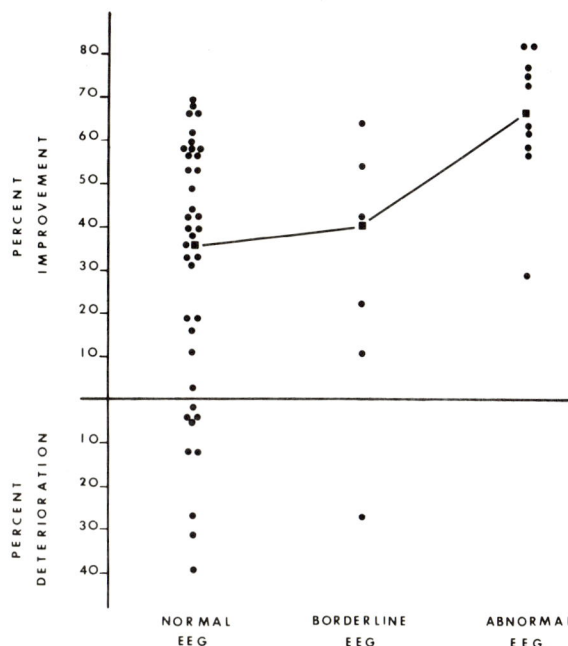

Fig. 4. Percentage of change in teacher rating scale following methylphenidate treatment in MBD children with (1) normal EEG, (2) borderline EEG, and (3) abnormal EEG findings.

the effect of the number of soft sign categories upon the percentage of patients in each group that obtained a good response to treatment (Table 2). A patient had to have 30% or more improvement in the teacher's rating scale in order to be considered as showing a good response.

Considering only patients with a normal or borderline EEG, 59% of the subjects who had soft signs in two or less categories improved, whereas 75% of the patients with soft signs in three to five categories improved following methylphenidate treatment. Then considering only patients with an abnormal EEG, 83% of the subjects with soft signs in two or less categories improved, whereas 100% of those patients with soft signs in three to five categories improved.

When we hold constant the effect of the neurologic findings, we can examine the effect of the EEG findings. Among patients with soft signs in two or less categories, 59%

Table 2. Percentage of Patients Improved (30% or Greater Improvement in Teacher Rating Scale) Following Methylphenidate Treatment in Each of Four Groups of MBD Children

Neurologic	Type of EEG		
	Normal and Borderline	Abnormal	Totals
0–2 Soft sign categories	$\frac{22}{37}$ 59%	$\frac{5}{6}$ 83%	$\frac{27}{43}$ 63%
3–5 Soft sign categories	$\frac{6}{8}$ 75%	$\frac{5}{5}$ 100%	$\frac{11}{13}$ 85%
Totals	$\frac{28}{45}$ 62%	$\frac{10}{11}$ 91%	

of the subjects with a normal EEG were improved, whereas 83% of the patients with an abnormal EEG improved following treatment. In those patients with soft signs in three or more categories, 75% of the subjects with a normal EEG improved, whereas 100% of the subjects with an abnormal EEG improved. If an abnormal EEG is considered to be a better indicator of brain dysfunction than soft neurologic signs, then groups of patients can be ranked from the group with the least evidence of brain dysfunction to the group with the most evidence of brain dysfunction (Table 2). The ranking from lowest to highest evidence of brain dysfunction would then be in the following order: (1) normal EEG and 0-2 soft sign categories; (2) normal EEG and 3-5 soft sign categories; (3) abnormal EEG and 0-2 soft sign categories; and (4) abnormal EEG and 3-5 soft sign categories. Also when we thus rank the groups in order of increasing evidence of brain dysfunction, the probability of a good response is lowest in group one (59%), next highest in group two (75%), next highest in group three (83%), and highest in group four (100%).

Although these trends are all in the predicted direction, none of the group differences are statistically significant. However, the correlation between the group ranking based upon the evidence of brain dysfunction and upon probability of response to treatment is $r = 1.0, p < 0.05$ (Spearman rank order correlation).

EXPERIMENT II

This is a study of auditory-evoked cortical responses in 31 MBD children and in 21 normal subjects matched for age and sex.

Method

Subject Selection and Evaluation: The method of subject selection and evaluation for this study was exactly the same as for Experiment I.

Details of the experimental procedure for the auditory evoked cortical response study have been reported elsewhere.[16]

Results

The mean age for both the 31 MBD and the 21 normal control subjects was 7 yr, 9 mo. The mean full scale WISC IQ was 118 for the control group and 104 for the MBD group. Thus, the controls had significantly ($p<0.001$) higher IQs. That the two groups differed significantly on many parent interview items and on teacher rating scales has been reported elsewhere.[15]

The typical average evoked response consists of a large negative-positive (N_1-P_2) wave beginning at around 100 msec, followed by a large positive-negative (P_2-N_2) wave. These three components of the evoked response we have designated as P_1, N_1, and P_2, and their peak-to-peak differences were selected to compare MBD and normal controls (Fig. 5). The early positive response (P_1), clearly seen in this figure, was not always easily identifiable in all records, especially at the faster stimulus rate, and therefore was not analyzed.

When peak-to-peak amplitudes of the N_1-P_2 and P_2-N_2 components of the evoked response at the slow (one stimulus every 2.5 sec) rate are compared in the two groups, it can be seen that the MBD group have smaller evoked response amplitudes (Table 3). When the latencies are compared we see that the MBD children have a longer latency of the N_1 peak, but a shorter latency of the late N_2 peak. When the amplitudes and

EEG ISSUES

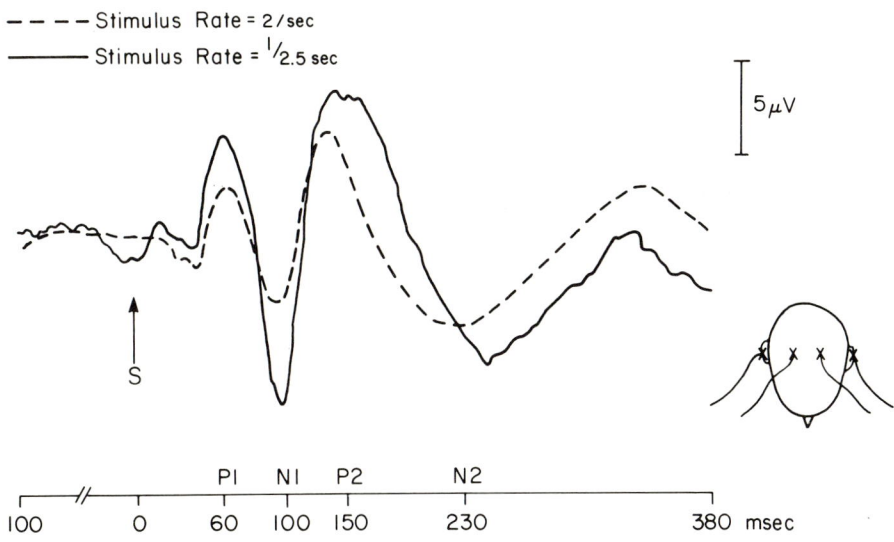

Fig. 5. Typical average auditory evoked cortical response. Positivity at vertex electrode gives upward deflection. Response at slow stimulus rate is average of approximately 400 individual responses, and response at fast stimulus rate is average of approximately 1600 individual responses.

Table 3. Comparison of Auditory Evoked Response Amplitudes and Latencies at the Slow Stimulus Rate (1/2.5 sec) Between MBD and Matched Normal Control Children

	No.	Amplitude (μV)		Latency (msec)		
		N_1-P_2	P_2-N_2	N_1	P_2	N_2
MBD	31	8.08	14.1	106	174	238.5
Control	21	13.6	19.7	94.7	184	246.4
p Value		0.002	0.002	0.01	NS	0.001

latencies of the average evoked response at the fast (two stimuli per sec) rate are compared, it can be seen that, as was found for the evoked response at the slow stimulus rate, the MBD group have smaller amplitudes of the evoked cortical response (Table 4). The MBD children also have longer latencies of both the N_1 and P_2 components of this evoked response. The amplitude measurement that best differentiates the two groups is the late positive P_2 wave (peak-to-base level) of the evoked response at the fast stimulus rate. In fact, when MBD children were compared with the normal controls on this late positive component, we found that 19 of 32 (60%) had smaller amplitudes than did any of the normal controls (Fig. 6). Age and IQ were not found to be correlated with either amplitude or latency of the evoked responses.

Table 4. Comparison of Auditory Evoked Response Amplitudes and Latencies at the Fast Stimulus Rate (2/sec) Between MBD and Normal Control Children

	No.	Amplitude (μV)			Latency (msec)		
		N_1-P_2	P_2-N_2	P_2	N_1	P_2	N_2
MBD	32	2.9	9.1	3.7	105.5	145.4	224
Control	23	5.37	12.49	5.8	85.5	137.8	229
p Value		0.001	0.001	0.0002	0.001	0.05	NS

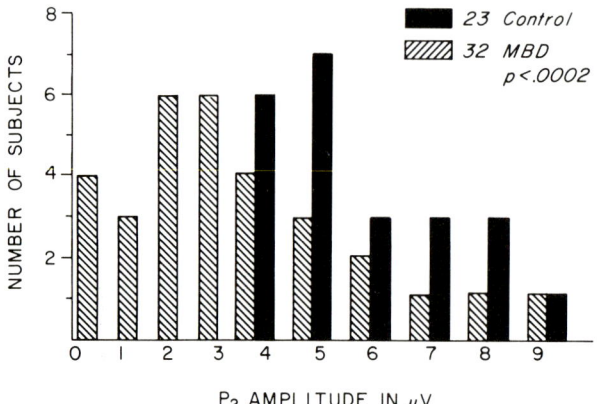

Fig. 6. Comparison of amplitude of P_2 component of average evoked cortical response between MBD children and control subjects.

DISCUSSION

Ohlrich et al. have reported that auditory evoked response latencies decrease and amplitudes increase with age in the first year of life.[8] Decreasing latency and increasing amplitude of the auditory evoked response throughout childhood had been reported.[17] Our findings that MBD children have longer latencies and smaller amplitude evoked responses than do normal age-matched controls suggest that these differences may represent a delayed central nervous system maturation in the MBD child. Although the MBD and control groups were not matched on IQ, the evoked response latency differences cannot be accounted for on the basis of IQ differences, since a significant correlation between IQ and latency was not found. Both the long latency and low amplitude evoked cortical responses, and the greater response to treatment in the MBD group with abnormal EEG and neurologic examination suggest an underlying neurophysiologic basis for the disorder in many MBD children.

The most common clinical EEG abnormality found by us and reported by others is an excessive amount of slow wave activity. This abnormality, like the increased latency of evoked response, is consistent with delayed maturation of the nervous system.

The most common type of abnormality found on neurologic examination (poor coordination) is also consistent with delayed maturation of the nervous system. If the pathophysiology underlying the disturbed behavior of the MBD child is delayed maturation rather than brain injury, as we believe, there is hope that, given enough time, the child will outgrow the condition. However, the condition is known to persist throughout childhood.[20] Further, these children if untreated develop secondary behavior and emotional problems along with academic failure in many cases.[20] This being the case, even if the original problem eventually dissipates, we are left with an educationally handicapped and emotionally crippled individual with high risk for psychopathology in later life.[6]

Unlike the clinical EEG data reviewed earlier, the evoked cortical response measure may be of real help in the diagnosis of the MBD child. If used as the sole diagnostic test in the above study, it would have been correct 60% of the time.

Most studies of the predictive value of the clinical EEG in children with psychiatric disorders have shown it to be of little use.[12] However, a few studies of MBD have reported that evoked cortical responses,[15] soft neurologic signs,[7] and a combination of signs of organicity (such as history, neurologic examination, and clinical EEG[2]) may be of value in predicting response to stimulant drug treatment. This study presents evidence that an abnormal EEG or four or more soft sign categories on the neurologic examination predict a good response to treatment.

Since most of the patients with an abnormal or borderline EEG also had positive findings on the neurologic examination, a given patient's response may reflect the combined effect of these two abnormalities. When these two effects are studied separately by holding one variable constant, we find that the presence of three or more neurologic soft sign categories is associated with an increased probability of obtaining a good response independent of the patient's EEG. Also, when we hold constant the number of soft neurologic signs, the presence of an abnormal EEG is associated with an increased probability of a good response to treatment independent of the neurologic finding. The probability of obtaining a good response to treatment is enhanced somewhat more by an abnormal EEG finding than by the presence of three or more categories of neurologic soft signs (Table 2, Figs. 3 and 4).

However, it should be noted that even in those patients with the least evidence of brain dysfunction (normal neurologic examinations and normal EEGs), the probability of obtaining a good response to methylphenidate treatment is 60% (Fig. 2).

As clinicians, we are still left without being able to predict accurately which child will or will not respond to methylphenidate treatment. As in other fields of medicine, we have to balance the expected benefit with the risks of treatment. If we consider 30% or more improvement a good clinical response to treatment, then 70% of the entire group of 57 subjects improved. Twenty-one per cent were worse following treatment. One other consideration has to be weighed in deciding whether or not to utilize a particular treatment, and that is the possible deleterious effect of "no treatment," which is after all, a form of treatment. Follow-up studies indicate that MBD, if untreated, results in increased risk for psychopathology in later life, ranging from poor social adjustment, underachievement and scholastic failure, to juvenile delinquency and even in some cases, psychosis.[6,20]

SUMMARY AND CONCLUSIONS

Thirty-one MBD children were compared with 21 normal controls matched for age and sex. The MBD group were found to have significantly smaller amplitude and longer latency auditory-evoked cortical responses. MBD children with soft signs in four or more categories respond with significantly more improvement ($p < 0.01$) to methylphenidate treatment than do MBD children with no soft signs. MBD children with abnormal EEGs have significantly more improvement ($p < 0.001$) than do MBD children with normal EEGs. There was a significant correlation between the amount of brain dysfunction (as judged by EEG and neurologic examination) and the probability of response to methylphenidate treatment. These findings suggest a neurophysiological basis for MBD and are consistent with a theory of delayed maturation of the central nervous system. Both the neurologic and the EEG examinations have a significant role to play in the treatment of the MBD child. Seventy per cent of the 57 MBD children obtained a good clinical response to methylphenidate treatment and 20% were worse.

ACKNOWLEDGMENT

The author wishes to thank Drs. Ronald Saul, Leonard Lesser, Dennis Cantwell, Alvin Yusin, and Robert Podosin for their assistance; Allison Burleigh, Grigor Atoian, Janet Anding, and Sandra Burton for help in collecting and analyzing the data; and Dr. Michael Dawson for his critical suggestions.

REFERENCES

1. Capute, A. J., Niedermeyer, E. F. L., and Richardson, F.: The electroencephalogram in children with minimal cerebral dysfunction. Pediatrics 41:1104, 1968.
2. Conrad, G. W., and Insel, J. B.: Anticipating the response to amphetamine therapy in the treatment of hyperkinetic children. Pediatrics 40:96, 1967.
3. Gibbs, E. L., Gillen, H. W., and Gibbs, F. A.: Disappearance and migration of epileptic foci in childhood. Am. J. Dis. Child. 88:596, 1954.
4. Hughes, J. R.: Electroencephalography and learning disabilities. *In* Myklebust, H. R. (Ed.): Progress in Learning Disabilities, Vol. II. New York, Grune & Stratton, 1971.
5. Klinkerfuss, G. H., Lange, P. H., Weinberg, W. A., and O'Leary, J. L.: Electroencephalographic abnormalities of children with hyperkinetic behavior. Neurology 15:889, 1965.
6. Menkes, M. M., Rowe, J. S., and Menkes, S. H.: A twenty-five year follow-up study on the hyperkinetic child with minimal brain dysfunction. Pediatrics 39:393, 1967.
7. Millichap, G.: Stimulant drugs, activity level and neurological dysfunction. Presented at Abbott Laboratories Symposium on the Clinical Use of Stimulant Drugs in Children, Key Biscayne, Florida, March 1972.
8. Ohlrich, E. S., and Barnet, A. B.: Auditory-evoked responses during the first year of life. Electroencephalogr. Clin. Neurophysiol. 32:161, 1972.
9. Paine, R. S., Werry, J. S., and Quay, H. C.: A study of minimal cerebral dysfunction. Dev. Med. Child Neurol. 10:505, 1968.
10. Pond, D. A.: The EEG in pediatrics. *In* Hill, J. D. N., and Parr, G. (Eds.): Electroencephalography: A Symposium on Its Various Aspects (ed. 2). London, MacDonald, 1963.
11. Ritvo, E. R., Ornitz, E. M., Walter, R. D., and Haley, J.: Correlation of psychiatric diagnoses and EEG findings: A double-blind study of 184 hospitalized children. Am. J. Psychiatry 126:988, 1970.
12. Rutter, M., Graham, P., and Yule, W.: A neuropsychiatric study in childhood. London, C.D.M. 35 and 36, Spastics International Medical Publications, 1970, p. 208.
13. Satterfield, J.H.: Unpublished data.
14. —, Atoian, G. E., Brashears, G. C., Burleigh, A. C., and Dawson, M. E.: Electrodermal studies in minimal brain dysfunction children. Presented at Abbott Laboratories Symposium on the Clinical Use of Stimulant Drugs in Children, Key Biscayne, Florida, March 1972.
15. —, Cantwell, D. P., Lesser, L. I., and Podosin, R. L.: Physiological studies of the hyperkinetic child: I. Am. J. Psychiatry 128:1418, 1972.
16. —, Lesser, L. I., Saul, R. E., and Cantwell, D. P.: EEG aspects in the diagnosis and treatment of minimal brain dysfunction. Ann. N. Y. Acad. Sci., in press.
17. Schenkenberg, T.: Visual auditory and somatosensory evoked responses of normal subjects from childhood to senescence. Unpublished Ph.D. Thesis.
18. Stevens, J. R., Sachdev, K., and Milstein, V.: Behavior disorders of childhood and the electroencephalogram. Arch. Neurol. 18:160, 1968.
19. Stewart, M. A., Thach, B. T., and Freidin, M. R.: Accidental poisoning and the hyperactive child syndrome. Dis. Nerv. Syst. 31:403, 1970.
20. Weiss, G., Minde, K., Werry, J. S., Douglas, V., and Nemeth, E.: The hyperactive child: VIII. Five year follow-up. Arch. Gen. Psychiatry 24:409, 1971.
21. Wender, P. H.: Minimal Brain Dysfunction in Children. New York, Wiley & Sons, 1971.
22. Wikler, A., Dixon, J. F., and Parker, J. B., Jr.: Brain function in problem children and controls: Psychometric, neurological, and electroencephalographic comparisons. Am. J. Psychiatry 127:634, 1970.

Lead Poisoning in Children: Neurologic Implications of Widespread Subclinical Intoxication

Herbert L. Needleman, M.D.

OF THE MANY CAUSES of impaired brain function, exogenous toxins should be among those agents easiest to identify, understand, and remedy. Lead is such an agent, one whose toxic significance has been recognized since antiquity. Yet, it remains a major threat to the brains and futures of thousands of urban American children.

The number of children known to be lead poisoned, who as a result often have sustained profound neurologic and psychologic sequelae, is dwarfed by a much larger group of children with unrecognized elevated body-lead burdens. This paper will argue that this latter group of unidentified asymptomatic children probably has significant neurologic and psychologic impairment.

The toxic effects of lead were described as early as the second century B.C. by Nicander, the Greek poet-physician. Later, Pliny warned of the hazards in the use of lead pots in wine-making.[10] Colic and paralysis after ingestion or inhalation of lead were accurately detailed by Dioscorides in the first or second century A.D.[11] The use of lead in cider vats as the cause of the Devonshire colic was established by Sir George Baker in the 18th century,[37] and the dry gripes of lead colic in tinkers and printers were graphically described by Benjamin Franklin. Long after its recognition as an industrial disease, lead poisoning became recognized as a threat to the young when, in 1925, Joseph Aub described the syndrome of childhood lead poisoning.[2]

CHILDHOOD LEAD POISONING

Most of the classical cases of this disease in the United States are associated with ingestion of lead-bearing paint. Pica, the eating of nonfood substances, is common behavior in the first 2 yr of life. If a child is bored, perhaps hungry, and in a lead-bearing environment, he is likely to persist in the habit and ingest significant amounts of lead. Although titanium oxide replaced lead in interior paint after World War II, millions of American homes in the inner city have paint with concentrations of lead over 1% by weight. Because it is common practice to apply new paint over old, and because other constituents of paint volatilize with the passage of time, concentrations as high as 40% by weight have been measured in the paint of older homes. The maximum permissible adult intake of lead is 1 mg/day. One gram of paint containing 1% lead contains 10 mg —ten times that dose. Thus, small amounts of this nearly ubiquitous toxin, taken over periods even as short as 3 mo, can produce clinical lead poisoning.

The onset of the disease is insidious and the symptoms nondescript. Fatigue, pallor, anorexia, and irritability may be followed by abdominal pain, vomiting, and motor unsteadiness. Headache and drowsiness presage the more severe signs of encephalopathy: convulsions, stupor, and coma. In its early stages, there is little to separate the

---

Reprint requests should be addressed to Herbert L. Needleman, M.D., Children's Hospital Medical Center, 300 Longwood Avenue, Boston, Mass. 02115.

symptoms from those of other less serious diseases of childhood. Undoubtedly, many of these children with milder symptoms of intoxication do not see a physician, and many who do are incorrectly diagnosed and treated. It is these children with unidentified lead poisoning, and the possible cost of intoxication to them, that are the issues in this paper.

Lead is stored in bone, liver, kidney, muscle, and the brain. It interferes with sulfhydryl groups on enzymes. The best-studied activity is its interference with heme synthesis at a number of loci, most notably by inhibiting delta-aminolevulinic acid dehydrase (ALA-D). The activity of this enzyme, measured in vitro, is depressed by lead at all levels of concentration.[13]

Clinical lead poisoning produces anemia, and often renal abnormalities, but its most important effects occur in the central nervous system. Pentschew's[30] postmortem examinations of brains of children who died from the acute disease demonstrated widespread encephalopathy, with perivascular cuffing, and occasional granuloma formations. These pathologic changes were most marked in the cerebellum. Thirty per cent of the cases had cerebral edema.

The neuropsychologic sequelae of children known to have had the disease are frequent and often severe. Byers and Lord[7] studied 20 children after recovery from lead poisoning, 9 of whom were felt to be free of encephalopathy. All were judged to be recovered at the time of discharge. All but one child were in the process of failing when followed in school; a high percentage were reported to be having difficulty in spatial tasks, were impulsive, and had short attention spans.

Mellins and Jenkins[19] found that 11 of 15 children treated for plumbism later had impaired visual-motor coordination and displayed irritability, emotional instability, and negativism. Bradley and Baumgartner,[6] using the Bender Gestalt Test, found visual-motor disturbances in 12 of 18 children treated for lead encephalopathy whose IQs were normal. Smith[38] studied the EEG records of children who recovered from lead poisoning, and found abnormal tracings in six of ten children who presented with encephalopathy. Only three of these children had clinical evidence of seizures, suggesting that the EEG may be of use in detecting occult neurologic damage in cases of plumbism, when seizures are not evident. Perlstein and Attala[31] followed 425 cases of diagnosed lead poisoning, and found neuropsychologic sequelae in 39%. Of those children whose initial onset was marked by encephalopathy, 82% had sequelae, most notably recurrent seizures and mental retardation. Of 59 children who had no symptoms at the time of diagnosis, and who were identified either inadvertently or because a sibling had the disease, five children (9%) were found to be mentally retarded.

Moncrief[21] studied 210 institutionalized children with unselected mental retardation, and found that the incidence of elevated blood lead levels was 45%; in normal controls the incidence was 2.5%. This study should not be taken to mean that lead was the primary etiologic agent in 45% of the hospital population, since a retarded child might develop pica as a secondary symptom. Still, the question of silent lead intoxication as a cause of retardation is raised, but left unanswered, by these data.

SIGNIFICANCE OF BLOOD LEAD LEVELS

The concentration of lead in whole blood presently is the generally accepted standard of exposure. Levels above 40 μg/100 ml are considered evidence of abnormal body burden. While most cases of clinical disease are associated with blood levels above 80 µg/100 ml, children with manifest signs and symptoms have been reported with blood lead levels below 50 µg/100 ml.[5,9]

A disturbingly high proportion of urban children carry blood levels that reach the range currently defined as toxic. In large-scale screening studies in New York City, 28.7% of ostensibly healthy children under 6 yr of age were found to have blood levels greater than 40 µg/100 ml, and 5.9% greater than 60 µg/100 ml. Similar data have been reported in other major cities.[22] It is estimated that 250,000 American children between the ages of 1 and 6 yr have elevated blood levels.[26] It is pertinent to ask how many of these children have cognitive impairment, behavior disorders, academic failure, or neurologic deficit related to the presence of this toxin.

The designation of 40 µg/100 ml as a threshold level below which no biologic damage is assumed to occur deserves reexamination. A single blood level is a static measurement of a number of dynamic forces: intake, excretion, and sequestration in tissue. It ignores differences in susceptibility of the host to lead. Such differences may derive from age, constitutional factors, nutritional status, and the presence of other disease processes that also compromise brain function.

While aminolevulinic acid excretion in the urine—one index of biologic interference due to lead—only begins to appear in significant amounts when the blood lead concentrations are greater than 40 µg/100 ml, depression of red cell ALA-D activity is found at levels well below 40 µg/100 ml. Nieburg et al. studied 420 children and found 19 who had depressed red cell ALA-D activity and normal blood lead concentrations.[25] When these children were treated with calcium versenate, a chelating agent that causes lead to be excreted, excessive amounts of lead in their urine were produced. This study clearly demonstrates that in certain cases, children can store abnormally large amounts of lead without its being reflected in their bloodstream.

These studies taken in sum indicate that the blood lead level is an imperfect index of exposure and damage to the organism, and suggest that damage can occur at levels below those accepted as safe. Even so, a formidable percentage of urban children, assumed to be asymptomatic, have blood levels of lead at concentrations associated with hazard to their nervous systems. Kotok's recent study[15] of 24 children with elevated blood lead levels reported no significant differences in developmental status when compared to controls matched for socioeconomic class. Aside from the small sample size, and coarse-grained developmental testing instrument (Denver Developmental Screening Test), the conclusion of the study should be viewed with skepticism, since the mean blood lead level of the subjects taken as controls was 38 µg/100 ml.

David and coworkers[8a] recently reported elevated blood lead levels and increased urinary excretion of lead after challenge with penicillamine in a group of children being treated for hyperactivity compared to nonhyperactive controls from the same clinic.

TOOTH LEAD LEVELS

Other tissues store lead and reflect past exposure. Altshuler[1] demonstrated significant elevations in lead content of deciduous teeth of children who had succumbed to lead poisoning. Needleman, Tuncay, and Shapiro studied 109 deciduous teeth shed by ostensibly normal children, 69 from the urban "lead belt" of Philadelphia, and 40 from children in the suburbs, where lead poisoning is almost unknown.[24] The mean tooth lead level for urban children was 51.1 ± 109 µg/g and for suburban children, 11 ± 14.8 μg/g, (Fig. 1). Three teeth obtained from children who had recovered from lead poisoning had values of 110, 92, and 67 μg/g. Fifteen children, or 22% of the urban groups, had tooth lead levels equal to or exceeding these values.

Studies employing electron microprobe analysis, and microdissection of the teeth have shown increased concentrations in the secondary dentine adjacent to the pulp. This area is continuously laid down, and concentrations of lead here reflect postnatal exposure.

Recently, we analyzed this zone in the teeth of 9 children known to have had lead poisoning, 20 children from the Boston suburbs, and 17 children from Iceland. The results were 601 ±225 μg/g, 84.4 ±56.6 μg/g and 35 ±29.8 μg/g, respectively.[23] This supports the validity of this issue as an index of past exposure, and suggests that suburban American children may have increased body-lead burdens.

One-thousand teeth from asymptomatic children enrolled in the Philadephia school

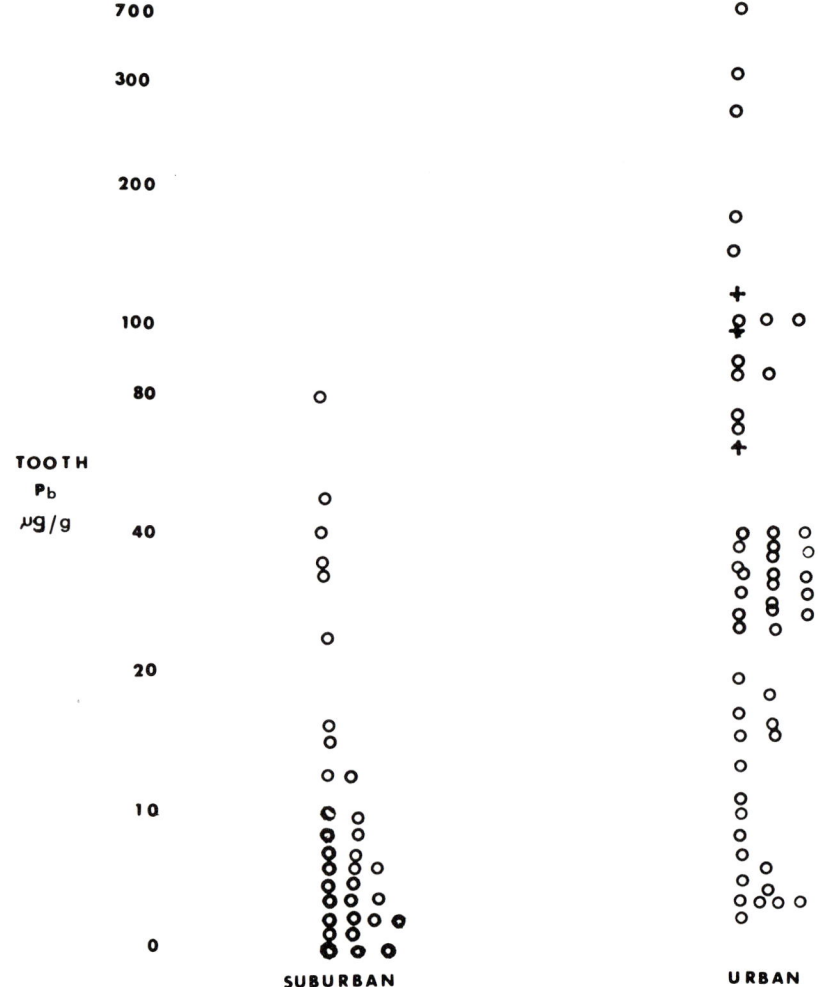

Fig. 1. Tooth lead levels of asymptomatic urban and suburban Philadelphia school children. The three crosses represent teeth from children who were known to have lead poisoning. (Adapted from Needleman et al.[24])

system are currently being analyzed. The study of the neuropsychologic performance of these children, and its relation to body burden of lead as reflected in teeth, while controlling for other environmental factors, may clarify the actual incidence of subclinical intoxication.

RELATIONSHIP OF AGE TO VULNERABILITY

The increased vulnerability of the very young organism to lead has been shown in a number of experimental studies, and suggests that fetuses in utero may also be at risk. Bell[4] demonstrated that immature tadpoles died in concentrations of lead that were not lethal to mature tadpoles. Schroeder[35] administered lead to pregnant mice and rats at levels insufficient to produce symptoms in the mothers. He found shortened life span, reduced litter size, and runting. Refeeding of lead to offspring caused the strains to die out after the second generation.

The feeding of lead to nursing mother mice[18] and to offspring pups after weaning produced dose-related decreases in brain size, retarded myelination, and cerebellar maturation in the pups. Millar[20] administered lead to pregnant female rats, and found that their nursed offspring had significantly decreased blood ALA-D levels and parallel decreases in brain ALA-D. Rats fed at lower levels produced offspring with mean blood lead levels of 30 μg/100 ml, and smaller decreases in brain ALA-D levels.

In clinical studies of humans, similar effects have been observed. Women exposed to lead through industrial sources are known to demonstrate decreased fertility and increased abortion rates. Ingestion of lead in bootleg whiskey by pregnant women has produced defective offspring.[27] Lead is known to cross the placenta,[3] and has been found in the cord blood of newborn infants delivered in Boston[34] and New York City[32] in concentrations ranging from 10-39 μg/100 ml. The effects of lead in these concentrations during the embryogenesis of the central nervous system have not yet been measured, but are a subject for troubled conjecture.

An analogy with phenylketonuria in pregnant women is instructive with respect to the question of toxic intrauterine exposure. Recently, numerous observers[8,16,28,33] have reported that women with phenylketonuria have given birth to offspring who, while genetically normal, were mentally retarded. These women were treated with dietary restriction in early life, and maintained low enough blood phenylalanine levels to allow their nervous systems to develop. In adult life, they were able to eat a normal diet and allow the blood phenylalanine levels to rise, without injury to their mature nervous system. The raised concentrations of phenylalanine that ensued and were transferred across the placenta were, however, toxic to the brains of the fetuses. In a similar manner, levels of lead insufficient to cause symptoms in the mother may produce effects in the fetus.

OTHER SOURCES OF LEAD

While ingestion of paint remains a major cause of lead poisoning, the studies mentioned above direct attention to other possibilities. In the United States each year, 200,000 tons of lead are emitted into the atmosphere, 98% of this from the combustion of lead-containing gasoline. The consumption of lead for use in gasoline additives has increased by 65% over the past 10 yr, and more than quadrupled since 1943. Increases in ambient air lead levels measured from 1962-1969 in three major cities ranged from 33%-64% in Los Angeles, 25%-36% in Philadelphia, and 26%-33% in Cincinnati.[12]

Approximately 30% of inhaled lead of small particle size is absorbed in the respiratory tract. Blood lead levels of urban parking lot attendants, traffic policemen, and tunnel employees are substantially elevated compared to other occupations. Urban Philadelphians have twice the blood lead concentration of their suburban, noncommuting counterparts. It is reasonable, then, to expect that urban pregnant women have higher blood lead levels than rural mothers.

The levels of ambient air lead reported are measured in air-sampling stations and do not reflect those at the street level where children play and breathe. Accordingly, while the mean downtown atmospheric concentration for Los Angeles was 3 µg/cu m, concentrations of 23.6 µg/cu m in downtown traffic, and 38.0 µg/cu m on the freeway were measured.

Recently, McIntire and Angle[17] reported significantly higher blood lead levels in asymptomatic children attending school 0.2 miles from a battery plant than children attending school 0.7 miles from the same plant. The mean blood lead levels were 38.2 µg/100 ml and 27.0 µg/100 ml, respectively.

As a result of fallout from the atmosphere, urban dirt has now become dangerous. In Cincinnati, 25 ft from the roadway, the average lead concentration was 3397 µg/g; at 100 feet, 2825 µg/g. The ingestion by a child of as little as $\frac{1}{24}$ th of a teaspoon of urban dust daily over an 8-mo span could produce lead poisoning.[36]

CONCLUSIONS

Recognition of a disease begins with the identification of clusters of obvious, often dramatic symptoms. The percept is formed, and then broadened to include lesser forms of the process. The falling sickness of epilepsy was only later found to be etiologically related to petit mal and psychomotor equivalents, and the diagnostic rubric then extended. If a noxious agent produces unusual effects, the task of epidemiologic identification is made relatively easy. Had thalidomide produced mental retardation rather than the characteristic deformity of phocomelia, it might still be sold and ingested in Europe and the United States.

Minor degrees of perceptual and cognitive impairment, motor incoordination, and disturbances in attention can easily escape detection. The population of impoverished urban American children is known to have significantly higher prevalences of neurologic dysfunction[29] and learning disorders.[14] Among the constellation of chronic assaults on the nervous systems of these children are prematurity, perinatal disease, malnutrition, infection, anemia, and a systematic burdening of lead.

Lead in high doses can produce devastating neurologic residua, and it is logical to expect that lesser doses can lead to lesser, though significant, damage. The selection of a threshold concentration of blood lead, based upon the absence of stark signs and symptoms, cannot be taken to mean that insidious impairment does not occur.

The renewed controversy over race and intelligence generally has ignored this systematic distribution of lead among the urban poor. Environmental diseases can mock genetic mechanisms; lead poisoning runs in families.

Rarely do serious health threats present themselves to such ready detection and elimination. The answer is clear: identify the lead in the environment and remove it. Mass screening programs, while they have been useful in preventing death and encephalopathy, still are employing the child as a biologic detector of the agent. Current instrumentation is available to rapidly measure the lead in air, dirt, and on the walls before it enters the body.

While important work must be done to accurately fix the neurologic cost of lesser lead exposure, enough is known at present to provide a clear imperative for action. It is a formidably expensive task, requiring billions, not millions of dollars. Lead-bearing paint must be removed, collected, and disposed of in a safe manner. Alternate pigments and covering agents are available. The insertion of lead into the air must be ended, and our technology turned toward developing means of extracting lead from urban dirt and dust. The price of inaction is the abridged futures of unmeasured thousands of children.

REFERENCES

1. Altshuler, L. F., Halah, D. B., and Landing, B.: Deciduous teeth as an index of body burden of lead, J. Pediatr. 60:224, 1964.
2. Aub, J. C., Fairhall, L. T., Minot, A. S., and Resnikoff, P.: Lead Poisoning. Baltimore, Williams & Wilkins, 1926.
3. Barltrop, D.: Transfer of lead to the human foetus. In Barltrop, D., and Burland, W. L. (Eds.): Mineral Metabolism in Pediatrics. Philadelphia, F. A. Davis Co., 1969.
4. Bell, W. B.: Influence of lead on normal and abnormal cell growth. Lancet 1:267, 1924.
5. Berman, E.: The biochemistry of lead: Review of the body distribution and methods of lead determination. Clin. Pediatr. (Phila.) 5:287, 1966.
6. Bradley, J. E., and Baumgartner, R. J.: Subsequent mental development of children with lead encephalopathy as related to type of treatment. J. Pediatr. 53:311, 1958.
7. Byers, R. K., and Lord, E. E.: Late effects of lead poisoning on mental development. Am. J. Dis. Child. 66:471, 1943.
8. Coffelt, R. W.: Unexpected findings from a PKU newborn screening program. Pediatrics 34:889, 1964.
8a. David, D., Clark, J., and Voeller, K.: Lead and hyperactivity. Lancet 2:900, 1972.
9. Freeman, R.: Chronic lead poisoning in children: A review of 90 children diagnosed in Sydney 1948-1967. Med. J. Aust. 1:640, 1970.
10. Gilfillan, S. C.: Lead poisoning and the fall of Rome. J. Occup. Med. 7:53, 1965.
11. Hamilton, A., and Hardy, H. L.: Industrial Toxicology (ed. 2). New York, Hoeber, 1949.
12. Health Hazards of Lead. Environmental Protection Agency Report (mimeo.), 1972.
13. Hernberg, S., Nikkanen, J., Mellin, G., and Lilius, H.: Delta-aminolevulinic dehydrase as a measure of lead exposure. Arch. Environ. Health 21:140, 1970.
14. Kappelman, M. K., Kaplan, E., and Ganter, R. L.: A study of learning disorders in disadvantaged children. In Chess, S., and Thomas, A. (Eds.): Annual Progress in Child Psychiatry and Child Development. New York, Brunner-Mazel, 1970.
15. Kotok, D.: Development of children with elevated blood lead levels: A controlled study. J. Pediatr. 80:57, 1972.
16. Mabry, C. C., Denniston, J. C., and Coldwell, J. B.: Mental retardation in children of phenylketonuria mothers. N. Engl. J. Med. 275:1331, 1966.
17. McIntire, M., and Angle, C.: Air lead: Relation to lead in blood of Black school children deficient in glucose-6-phosphate dehydrogenase. Science 177:520, 1972.
18. Maker, H. S., Lehrer, G. M., and Slides, D. J.: The effect of lead on brain development. Trans. Am. Acad. Neurology, 1972, p. 92.
19. Mellins, R. B., and Jenkins, C. D.: Epidemiological and psychological study of lead poisoning in children. JAMA 158:15, 1955.
20. Millar, J. A., Cummings, R. L. C., Battistini, V., Carswell, F., and Goldberg, A.: Lead and delta-aminolevulinic acid dehydratase levels in mentally retarded children, and in lead-poisoned suckling rats. Lancet 2:695, 1970.
21. Montcrief, A. A., Koumides, O. P., Clayton, E. E., Patrick, A. D., Renwick, A. G. C., and Roberts, G. E.: Lead poisoning in children. Arch. Dis. Child. 39:1, 1964.
22. Mustalish, A.: Testimony given before Environmental Protection Agency, 1972.
23. Needleman, H., and Shapiro, I.: Lead in deciduous teeth: A marker of exposure in heretofore asymptomatic children. Proceedings of International Symposium on Environmental Health Aspects of Lead. Amsterdam, 1972.
24. —, Tuncay, O. C., and Shapiro, I. M.: Lead levels in deciduous teeth of urban and suburban American children. Nature 235:111, 1972.
25. Nieburg, P. I., Oski, B. F., Cornfeld, D., and Oski, F. A.: Red cell ALA-D activity as an index of body lead burden. Pediatr. Res. 6:366, 1972.
26. Oberle, M. W.: Lead poisoning: A preventable childhood disease of the slums. Science 165:991, 1969.

27. Palmisano, P. A., Sneed, R. C., and Cassady, G.: Untaxed whiskey and fetal lead exposure. J. Pediatr. 75:869, 1969.

28. Partington, M. W.: Variations in intelligence in phenylketonuria. Can. Med. Assoc. J. 86:736, 1962.

29. Pasamanick, B., and Knobloch, H.: Epidemiologic studies on the complications of pregnancy and the birth process. *In* Caplan, G. (Ed.): Prevention of Mental Illness in Children. New York, Basic Books, 1961.

30. Pentschew, A.: Morphology and morphogenesis of lead encephalopathy. ACTA Neuropathologica 5:133, 1965.

31. Perlstein, M. A., and Attala, R.: Neurologic sequelae of plumbism in childhood. Clin. Pediatr. 5:292, 1966.

32. Rajegowda, B. K., Glass, L., and Evans, H. E.: Lead concentrations in newborn infants. J. Pediatr. 80:116, 1972.

33. Richards, B. W.: Maternal phenylketonuria. Lancet 1:829, 1964.

34. Scanlon, J.: Umbilical cord lead concentration. Am. J. Dis. Child. 121:325, 1971.

35. Schroeder, H. A., and Mitchener, M.: Toxic effects of trace elements on the reproduction of mice and rats. Arch. Environ. Health 23:102, 1971.

36. Shy, C. M., Hammer, D. I., Goldberg, H. E., Newill, V. A., and Nelson, W. C.: Health hazards of environmental lead. In-house Technical Report, Community Research Branch, Bureau of Air Pollution Sciences, Environmental Protection Agency, 1971.

37. Singer C., and Underwood, E. A.: A Short History of Medicine. New York, Oxford University Press, 1962.

38. Smith, H. D., Balkner, R. L., Corney, T., and Majors, W. J.: The sequelae of pica with and without lead poisoning. Am. J. Dis. Child. 105:609, 1963.

Identification and Diagnosis of Children With Learning Disabilities: An Interdisciplinary Study of Criteria

Helmer R. Myklebust, Ed.D.

An extensive investigation was undertaken of criteria relating to identification, diagnosis, and treatment of learning-disability children. The psychoeducational evaluation showed that these children were disturbed in cognitive processes, especially as they pertain to converting auditory information into visual equivalents. The ophthalmologic findings were negative, but the electroencephalographic and neurologic studies revealed a higher incidence of abnormal signs. Although definitive patterns did not emerge, except psychoeducationally, neurologic information is critical to identification and diagnosis of learning disabilities.

D ESIGNATION OF CHILDREN as having a learning disability gradually has come into common practice. It seems there was a void, as though there were many children for whom there was no suitable terminology—an unclassifiable group. With the term "learning disability," a classification became available; there was a new way to refer to a significant number of exceptional children.

More than that, many clinicians, behavioral scientists, and educators needed a different way to view certain children. For some time it was thought that children with limitations could be served best when categorized in terms of end products; hence, the classifications of mentally retarded, emotionally disturbed, and others came into being. These designations served useful purposes until other vital considerations arose. These considerations related not so much to *what the child was,* but *how he functioned*—not so much to *end product,* but to how *processes were impeded.* As a term, learning disability gave impetus to this significant shift on the part of a number of disciplines. Now clinicians could stress, not only *what,* but *how* processes had been affected, with implications for treatment and remedial education.

The implications of this reorientation, from *what* to *how,* are of great importance to many children. But because of the widespread consequences, controversies ensued. In special education, there was concern regarding the inclusiveness of the concept, with questions as to whether it comprised the mentally retarded and emotionally disturbed. In psychiatry, a concern persisted regarding the precise interactions between emotional disturbances and learning disabilities. Similar questions were raised by psychologists and reading specialists.

Such developments might have been anticipated because they often follow initiation of new terminology. However, when overgeneralization occurs, the benefits to specialists and children are lost; a category that becomes unduly inclusive ceases to be meaningful. The alternative to overgeneralization is imposition of criteria, and definition in terms of relevancy. When this is done, the benefits often extend beyond a specific population, even to the normal. This has been demonstrated by the designa-

---

This investigation was made possible by USPHS Contract 108-65-142.

Reprint requests should be addressed to Helmer R. Myklebust, Ed.D., College of Education, University of Illinois at Chicago Circle, Box 4348, Chicago, Ill. 60680.

tions of infantile autism, childhood aphasia, and childhood dyslexia, all of which led to more awareness of the impositions that must be considered in serving the needs of children.

Most workers agree that the term "learning disability" has served these purposes to advantage. A new designation was imperative, as was the shift in emphasis from product to process. Nevertheless, questions have been raised, and these reflect varying opinions. Many attempts have been made to define more clearly what the new designation was to mean, and how it could be applied to greatest advantage.[1] However, these questions persist, sometimes urgently; for example, clarification is necessary to obtain suitable legislation. Medical and behavioral scientists continue to question to whom this designation should be applied—who, precisely, is the child with a learning disability. Until there is further agreement, the problems of identification, diagnosis, and management cannot be dealt with expeditiously. Involved, of course, is the need to establish criteria.

A STUDY OF CRITERIA

To provide objective data, an investigation was undertaken with support from the Neurological and Sensory Diseases Program, USPHS. This study, covering a period of approximately 4 yr (1965-69), was conducted by a group of behavioral and medical scientists, and involved cooperation from many parents, children, and public schools.

The Plan

The research paradigm served as a guideline. Children, of selected ages, who were enrolled in the participating schools but who were not achieving at expected levels although the learning opportunities were good, formed the experimental population. The approach was not one of beginning with clinical, disease-related referrals, but, rather, the fundamental criterion was underachievement. This necessitated screening all children in the stipulated grades to identify those not performing at expected levels. These underachievers were to be evaluated neurologically, electroencephalographically, educationally, psychologically, and ophthalmologically. Diagnostic criteria were to be established for each of these critical disciplines, as well as for all of them combined.

Interpretation of the data should be made in terms of this paradigm. The children in the experimental group were identified only by their educational underachievement. The research team was asked to provide diagnostic criteria for children unsuccessful in learning; they had not been previously identified as hyperkinetic, retarded, or emotionally disturbed. The research task, therefore, differed from that imposed when children are selected from pediatric, psychiatric, or other clinical populations. The purpose was to investigate deficits in learning in a manner that isolated these deficits as much as possible. Thus, social disadvantage and lack of opportunity also were minimized. The assumption was that if criteria could be established for this inclusive type of population, these criteria could be used with all types of school populations.

Definition and Design

To conduct such an extensive investigation, it was necessary to limit participation to a few disciplines: ophthalmology, pediatric neurology, electroencephalography, education, and psychology. Moreover, a basic task was to define educational underachievement. Criteria such as one or two grades below average have proved untenable in research, and expectancy usually has been defined only in terms of IQ. To resolve this problem, the learning quotient (LQ) was evolved by Myklebust.[5] This quotient is a ratio between *achievement and expectancy;* it is based on chronologic age and years of schooling in addition to IQ. Thus, expectancy is an average of mental ability, age, and school experience. Inclusion of life age (physiologic maturity) and extent of schooling made it possible to view expectancy as a ratio between potential and educational achievement.

When interpreting the results of this investigation, it is necessary to bear in mind that the LQ does not represent the child's potential for learning. Rather, it is a score that indicates the extent to which he is achieving his potential. An LQ can be computed for any type of learning that can be measured objectively. For example, an LQ can be derived for level of achievement in reading (silent, oral, paragraph meaning, etc.), for facility with written language, as well as in arithmetic and other aspects of school learning.

Using the LQ, a learning disability was defined as a discrepancy between actual achievement and expected level of attainment. When this discrepancy exceeded 10% (LQ below 90), the child was classified as an underachiever. This criterion obviated concern with whether he was viewed as an underachiever by the school; bright children often pass their grades even though achieving below their potential.

The research design was stringent in other respects. Because normative data were largely unavailable, especially in regard to the medical areas, a control group was essential. Therefore, for every underachiever, a normal control child was selected. So that the control group would be as comparable as possible, these children were paired with underachievers and were selected from the same classrooms. Accordingly, underachievers and controls were of the same sex, same school and classroom, and were equivalent socioeconomically. The controls were studied in precisely the same manner as the experimentals. Hence, information was gathered on normal learners in relation to visual, neurologic, and EEG status. Evaluation of the children was made without the investigator's knowing whether the child was a normal learner or an underachiever.

All third and fourth graders in the four participating school systems were screened to determine the extent to which they were achieving at the expected level, as defined quantitatively by the LQ. The total number of children screened was 2767, of whom 2.28% were eliminated for low IQ or medical reasons. The basic population comprised 2704 children. On the basis of the screening tests, 15% of this population were identified as underachievers. These children and their paired controls were evaluated intensively to determine further the reasons for their failure to learn at the expected level.

THE INTENSIVE EVALUATION

The children identified as underachievers were scheduled, together with their controls, for an intensive evaluation as performed by each of the disciplines; this examination required approximately 2 days per child. The procedures for each are described briefly.

Psychologic-Educational Study

The psychoeducational study was performed by psychologists and specialists in learning disabilities. The test battery covered cognitive abilities in the areas of auditory and visual perceptual skills, expressive and receptive language (spoken, read, and written), academic achievement, verbal and nonverbal mental abilities, social perception, motor abilities, orientation in time and space, and social and emotional maturity. From this test battery, 47 scores were derived. To be classified as having a learning disability, the child had to attain an LQ of 89 or lower on one or more of 21 selected tests from this battery. To be included in the control sample, the child had to attain an LQ of 90 or above on all of the 21 test criteria.

However, other selective criteria were applied. Functional limits were established for sensory capacities, motor functions, emotional adjustment, and intelligence. Both experimental and control groups demonstrated normal hearing, normal vision (20/40), adequate emotional adjustment as determined by the CPQ (Cattell), an IQ of 90 or above on either the verbal or performance section of the WISC, and had no obvious motor disabilities. Because the degree of involvement was considered consequential to the results, two groups were established for the children having learning deficits. One, the *borderline* group, had LQs ranging from 85–89. The second, the *learning disability* group, had LQs of 84 or below. These groups were studied separately, each in comparison with its own control group.

Ophthalmologic Study

Vision and visual processes are related to success in learning, especially in learning to read. Various individuals and professional groups concerned with learning disabilities have emphasized the role of vision, sometimes to the exclusion of other dimensions. In view of its significance, ophthalmologic studies were made of all children selected for the intensive diagnostic phase of the investigation.

The ophthalmologic history covered all aspects related to the child's vision: birth defects, use of glasses, orthoptics, surgery, strabismus, and others. Vision was tested with and without glasses for each eye individually; this included testing for distance vision (20 ft) and near vision (14 in); normal was defined as 20/20 to 20/40, defective as 20/50 or below. Ocular coordination was examined by placing the Maddox Rod over the right eye while viewing a muscle light mounted on the wall 20 ft away with the left eye. The Maddox Wing test was used for determination of ocular alignment in the reading range. Notation was made of eso-, exo-, or hypertropia. Horizontal direction was considered normal if the measurements were between zero and five prism diopters; six prism diopters or more were designated as abnormal. In the vertical direction, one diopter or less was classified as normal, whereas more than one prism diopter was categorized as abnormal.

Refractive error was evaluated by retinoscopy approximately 30 min after instillation of two drops of 1% Mydriacel, administered 5 min apart. One diopter or less of hyperopia, myopia, or astigmatism was noted as normal. Hyperopia and myopia values in excess of one diopter were classified as abnormal, as was more than one diopter of astigmatism. The axis of the astigmatism also was recorded. Accommodation was determined individually for each eye, with a reading of 11–16 diopters viewed as normal, and ten or less as abnormal. Ocular dominance was determined by sighting through a 5-mm hole in the center of a cardboard held at arm's length in both hands.

The neuro-ophthalmologic examination included the following: *pupillary reaction*—direct and consensual, to light, with accommodation and equality noted; *corneal sensation*—a cotton wisp gently applied to the center of each cornea; *intactness* of the 3rd, 4th, and 6th cranial nerves—turning eyes to the right, left, up, and down by fixating on a light in the six cardinal gaze directions; *convergence*—fixation on a small symbol moved progressively closer toward the bridge of the nose until one of the eyes deviated, at which point the distance was recorded in millimeters; *visual field*—by the Harrington-Flocks visual screener; and *color vision*—by the Ishihara pseudochromatic plates.

Electroencephalographic Study

A primary objective was to ascertain the contributions of given disciplines to identification, diagnosis, and treatment of children with learning disabilities. Electroencephalography comprises a body of knowledge significant to study of minimal brain damage.[2,3] In the EEG investigation, the same research design was used as for the other aspects of the study. The EEG investigator read the record without knowledge of whether it was for an experimental or a control subject. The same reader read all of the records (inter- and intrareliability studies of his classifications had previously been made). After reading the record, he wrote a diagnostic report, including classification and discussion of the findings, positive and negative. The statistical analysis covered these clinical designations as well as the objective findings (see "Results" section).

Each child's head was measured with a millimeter ruler, and using the 10-20 International System of Electrode Placement, areas were marked for electrode application. The leads were placed on the scalp symmetrically at equal relative distances from each other. The electrodes (22) were secured by means of dried collodion around a 2 × 2-in gauze square placed over them. A conducting paste was applied over each area where activity was monitored.

Both referential (2) and bipolar (6) montages were used during the recording from an eight-channel EEG unit (Grass type 6 or Offner Type T). Effect of eye-opening and eye-closure was tested during several montages, and activation by hyperventilation (5 min) was assessed. The effect of repetitive photic stimulation also was determined; seven to eight different stimulating frequencies of 1-25/sec were used for durations of 8-10 sec each. Finally, a sleep record was obtained mainly to search for epileptiform activity.

Pediatric Neurologic Study

A principal frame of reference for this research was that minimal brain dysfunction was associated with certain types of deficits in learning. Thus, a basic objective was to gather data to clarify the characteristics of such relationships. As an area of specialization in medicine, neurology has demonstrated associations between behavioral anomalies and brain dysfunctions, but this knowledge pertains mainly to adults. During the past two decades, neurologists have extended the concept of brain dysfunctions to include subtle deviations in learning, including all age levels, even young children.

Because of this new emphasis, a specialty within a specialty developed—pediatric neurology. Because of the possibility that minimal brain dysfunction is a significant contributor to the population of learning-disability children, and because of the potential contribution of pediatric neurology to identification and treatment of this group, this discipline was included. Accordingly, a pediatric-neurologic examination was made of all subjects: those who failed the screening tests, and the controls. Consistent with the research design, the neurologist examined each child without knowing whether he was a member of the learning disability group or the control group. The examination covered mainly the following: *height and weight*—measured and compared to expected values; *head circumference*—circumference and shape noted, and auscultation performed at the temporal areas, over the eyes, over the carotid arteries, and at the suboccipital areas bilaterally; *facial characteristics*—deviations of the eyes and ears in terms of mandibulofacial dysostoses; *dentition*—irregularity, presence of malocclusion, caries, and dysplasia of enamel; *nose, mouth and pharynx*—particular attention to features of the palate; *neck*—length, webbing, and other abnormalities; *blood pressure*—using a children's cuff, several readings made and the mean recorded; *heart*—femoral and dorsalis pedis arteries palpated and inequality or weakness of pulse noted; *abdomen*—examined for deviations and palpated; *genitalia*—examined for deviations, as were the breasts and other secondary sexual characteristics; *skin*—the presence of angiomata, vitiligo spots, café au lait spots, neuromata and adenoma sebaceum noted; *spine*—configuration and characteristics of spinal dystrophia, with musculoskeletal system also examined; *motor functions*—walking, speed, steppage, arm swinging and turning. Station examined by standing with eyes closed, tandem walking, and standing on one foot, eyes open then closed; maintaining this position 7–10 sec was normal.

Reflexes—tendon responses. Clonus tested at ankles, knees, and wrists and plantar responses by Babinski, Chaddock, and Oppenheim. Abdominal reflexes by a sharp object at upper, mid, and lower segments of wall; cremasteric reflexes by sharp stimulus in reflexogenic zone of L-1. If sluggish, skin pinched to note total absence of reflex. Visceral reflexes by pupillary tests of light accommodation and consensual response; visceral responses by pilomotor characteristics and asymmetry. Similarly, vasomotor function noted by color of skin, warmth of skin on both sides of body and response to stroking. Pharyngeal action by a tongue depressor touching posterior pharyngeal wall.

Sensory functions—stereognosis by coins of different sizes; barognosis by weight judgments of half-dollar, quarter, and nickel; two-point discrimination by calipers, with distance of hands at 5 mm, applied to tips of fingers bilaterally and also on legs; skin writing by writing numbers on palms of hands and lower extremities; extinction by applying simultaneous stimuli; smell using vanilla, coffee, peppermint, and soap; vision by examination of fundi, noting status of disks, retinae, maculae, blood vessels, lens, and cornea; optokinetic nystagmus and 3rd, 4th, and 6th cranial nerves evaluated; taste by placing salt and sugar on anterior two-thirds of tongue; hearing acuity noted, and Rinne and Weber tests given.

Jaw and facial movements—jaw opening and movement from side to side, with facial movements scrutinized for asymmetries in emotional and volitional actions; *cranial nerves IX, X, and XI*—phonation, palatal elevation, and swallowing, and XI by shrugging shoulders and noting patterns of contraction in sternocleidomastoid muscles; *tongue*—size, atrophy, and fissures; protrusion and vertical and horizontal axes; and, lastly, *cerebellar function*—by rapid alternating movements, reflexes, past-pointing, and metria.

All evaluations were performed by the same examiner and the findings summarized in two parts. Part one covered the general physical examination and part two the neurologic. The neurologist classified his findings as normal or abnormal. The classification of abnormal was further categorized as *abnormal* or *suspect:* abnormal referred to "hard" signs and suspect to "soft" signs.

RESULTS

The psychoeducational tests covered six areas of behavior and learning: mental ability, educational achievement, motor ability, emotional adjustment, social maturity,

Table 1. Mental Age Scores for the Borderline Group (n = 116) and Controls (n = 116), and for the Learning-Disability Group (n = 112) and Controls (n = 112)

	Borderline Mean	SD	Control Mean	SD	t	Learning Disability Mean	SD	Control Mean	SD	t
WISC										
Information	10.3	1.8	11.3	1.9	3.90‡	9.9	1.5	11.0	1.7	4.83‡
Comprehension	9.5	2.3	10.1	2.2	1.91	9.6	1.7	9.8	2.1	0.90
Arithmetic	10.1	1.6	11.2	1.7	4.90	9.8	1.6	11.2	1.8	5.94‡
Similarities	11.1	2.5	11.9	2.7	2.18*	10.7	2.2	11.9	2.7	3.64‡
Vocabulary	10.3	2.1	11.6	2.0	4.52‡	10.1	1.8	11.5	2.0	5.58‡
Digit Span	9.7	3.0	11.3	3.3	3.90‡	10.1	3.0	11.3	3.3	2.92†
Mean Verbal	10.2	1.4	11.2	1.6	5.14‡	10.1	1.3	11.2	1.5	5.93‡
Picture Completion	9.9	2.9	10.4	2.7	1.39	10.1	2.8	10.4	2.8	0.73
Picture Arrangement	10.8	2.7	11.3	2.5	1.51	11.3	2.8	11.5	2.5	0.47
Block Design	10.6	2.6	11.5	2.5	2.86†	10.3	2.6	11.6	2.5	4.02‡
Object Assembly	10.6	2.9	11.0	2.6	1.22	10.2	2.9	11.1	2.6	2.48*
Coding	10.1	1.5	10.8	1.8	3.27†	10.2	1.3	10.8	1.7	3.11†
Mazes	10.0	2.7	10.5	2.7	1.19	10.0	2.8	10.6	2.6	1.77
Mean Performance	10.3	1.6	10.9	1.5	2.85	10.3	1.6	11.0	1.3	3.32‡
Detroit Test of Learning Aptitude										
Free Association	9.8	1.8	10.7	1.9	3.64‡	9.7	2.0	10.5	1.8	3.21†
Verbal Opposites	10.8	1.5	11.7	1.4	4.41‡	10.5	1.3	11.6	1.3	6.66‡
Words	7.9	2.3	9.2	2.4	4.19‡	8.0	2.2	9.2	2.6	3.64‡
Sentences	8.8	2.4	10.2	2.2	4.57‡	8.3	2.3	10.0	2.1	5.77‡
Oral Directions	9.9	2.1	11.0	2.0	4.15‡	9.5	2.1	11.0	2.1	5.13‡
Letters	10.0	1.5	11.0	1.9	4.45‡	9.6	1.4	10.9	1.8	6.24‡
Orientation	10.0	1.3	10.8	1.3	4.64‡	9.8	1.3	10.8	1.3	5.98‡
Designs	9.8	1.8	10.7	1.9	3.87‡	9.0	1.8	10.6	1.8	6.90‡
Other Measures										
Leiter	9.0	1.2	9.9	1.5	4.41‡	8.6	1.2	9.9	1.4	6.67‡
Kent D	10.7	2.2	11.8	1.9	3.87‡	10.1	2.0	11.7	1.8	6.34‡
Healy I	11.2	2.4	12.2	2.7	3.19†	10.9	3.1	12.6	2.8	4.52‡
Draw-A-Man	9.6	2.3	10.0	2.3	1.35	9.0	2.4	10.3	2.3	4.02‡

*$p < 0.05$; †$p < 0.01$; ‡$p < 0.001$.

and sensory acuity. (The specific tests administered are listed in Chapter IX, *Progress in Learning Disabilities,* Vol. II, edited by Myklebust.[6]) Forty-seven scores were derived and used in the statistical analyses. Each of the six areas of behavior is discussed separately and presented by group—borderline and learning disability groups.

Mental Ability

Several measures of mental ability were given and the results are presented in Table 1. Both groups, those classified as having minor learning deficits (borderline) and those with severe deficits (learning disability), were inferior to the controls on the tests of intelligence; the controls were slightly above average. The borderline and learning disability children did not differ from each other on the WISC; the average full scale score for the borderline children was 106, and for the learning disability, 104. They also were equivalent on the other tests of mental ability.

These results are enlightening. Although the children with deficiencies in learning were inferior to the controls, they were not below average in intelligence; their poor learning cannot be attributed to limitations in mental ability. Moreover, other analyses[6] revealed that those with disabilities in learning differed from the normals in cognitive functions. Therefore, their lowered mental test scores may reflect the handicap rather than actual differences in mental ability. This possibility is further supported by the additional information that the normals scored highest on verbal tests, whereas those with learning deficits were most successful on nonverbal tests.

Another significant aspect of these findings is that the borderline and learning disability populations did not differ from each other. Even though these groups did differ in extent of the deficit in learning, they were equivalent intellectually. These results indicate further that a learning disability may be severe, yet intelligence may fall at the average level. By implication, progress is being made in the definition of a learning disability. More specifically, for psychology and education, emphasis should be directed to disturbances in cognition, because increasingly there are indications that these are the primary bases of the deficit in learning. Although other psychologic factors may be of importance, it is the processes by which the child learns, and how these differ from the normal, that provide the basis for identification, diagnosis, and remediation.

Language and Educational Achievement

Most learning-disability children of school age are referred for clinical evaluation because of deficiencies in language or in some aspect of educational achievement. Therefore, the research paradigm provided for obtaining data on these facets, as well as on nonverbal aspects. The areas investigated included auditory receptive language, auditory expressive language, read and written language, arithmetic, and nonverbal learning. Auditory memory and ability to syllabicate also were appraised.

The results for language and educational achievement are presented in Table 2. The mean score for all areas of learning favored the controls, and the learning-disability group consistently fell below the borderline group. Nevertheless, the two experimental populations were equivalent in auditory language. The learning-disability group showed greater limitations in all the other areas: read and written language, arithmetic and nonverbal learning.

As shown by the results for auditory memory, the experimental groups were equal on this facet, though both were inferior to the controls. The significance of this deficit in auditory processing is revealed further by the syllabication test results. This test showed greatest inferiority for the learning-disability group, and was highly successful in differentiating between the normal and all the children with deficits in learning. Syllabication tests measure facility in determining the equivalence of auditory and visual word parts; what letters and word parts look like must be matched with what they sound like. The discriminant analysis (see below) disclosed that deficits in this cognitive function, more than any other aspect, differentiated between the experimental and control groups. Moreover, those with marked deficits in learning showed more limitations in this type of processing than those with minor deficiencies. In terms of identification, though both experimental groups showed deficits in auditory and visual learning (*intra*neurosensory processes), the most effective discriminator was facility in relating auditory and visual information (*inter*neurosensory processes). Even the degree of the involvement was clarified by this technique; it was more definitive than a battery of commonly used mental tests.

Emotional Adjustment

The Children's Personality Questionnaire was used to study emotional status. According to the standardized procedure, the items were read to the child, so the ability to read was not involved. An intricate statistical analysis of these data was made by Killen.[4] Except in minor respects, the mean scores for the control and experimental groups were identical, as were the standard deviations. Hence, as compared to the norms, all groups, control and experimental, fell within the average range. It is unlikely that the deficits in learning were attributable to emotional disturbance.

Social Maturity

The Vineland Social Maturity Scale was administered to ascertain the degree of self-sufficiency attained by each of the children; this scale is mainly a measure of ability to care for oneself (independence). The results showed both experimental groups to be inferior to the controls; the information is obtained through interviews with the parents; so school-learning aspects were minimal. The significance of these results is that they indicate the pervasive effect of the learning disability; it is not only a problem of academic learning. Program planning must include consideration of the generalized nature of this handicap.

Motor Ability

The Heath Railwalking test was given to evaluate locomotor coordination. Laterality was studied by throwing, kicking, and sighting tests. The findings revealed no relationships between laterality and deficits in learning.

INTERCORRELATION ANALYSIS

An intercorrelation analysis was performed to study the pattern of cognitive abilities and the relationship of these patterns to school learning; a detailed discussion of these results has previously been presented.[6] A major finding was that children with deficits in learning, irrespective of degree of involvement, had poor integration of verbal and nonverbal abilities. For example, coding and maze scores intercorrelated to a high degree with educational achievement in normal children, whereas this association was minimal for those deficient in learning. Similar differences appeared for "picture arrangement," "picture completion," and "block design."

To generalize, the intercorrelation analysis revealed less integration of cognitive

Table 2. Age Scores for Language and Educational Achievement for the Borderline Group (n = 116) and Controls (n = 116), and for the Learning-Disability Group (n = 112) and Controls (n = 112)

Test	Borderline Mean	SD	Control Mean	SD	t	Learning Disability Mean	SD	Control Mean	SD	t
Auditory Receptive										
Detroit Orientation	10.0	1.3	10.8	1.3	4.64‡	9.8	1.3	10.8	1.3	5.98‡
Kent D	10.7	2.2	11.8	1.9	3.87‡	10.1	2.0	11.7	1.8	6.34‡
Auditory Expressive										
Detroit Free Association	9.8	1.8	10.7	1.9	3.64‡	9.7	2.0	10.5	1.8	3.21†
Detroit Verbal Opposites	10.8	1.5	11.7	1.4	4.41‡	10.5	1.3	11.6	1.3	6.66‡
Oral PSLT Words per Sentence	11.6	3.0	12.5	3.2	2.25*	11.5	2.9	12.4	3.2	2.19*
Oral PSLT Abstract-Concrete	12.1	3.6	12.6	3.7	0.89	12.0	3.8	12.6	3.7	1.22
Reading										
Gates-MacGinitie Accuracy	9.6	2.1	11.1	2.6	4.47‡	8.6	1.4	11.1	2.9	7.36‡
Gates-MacGinitie Comprehension	9.3	1.6	11.2	2.1	6.86‡	8.3	1.2	11.0	2.1	10.48‡
Gates-MacGinitie Vocabulary	9.5	1.6	11.2	1.7	6.62‡	8.5	1.5	11.0	1.8	10.06‡
Written Language										
PSLT Total Words	9.3	2.3	10.1	2.9	2.57*	8.9	2.1	10.1	2.7	3.54‡
PSLT Words per Sentence	9.8	2.2	10.5	2.7	2.30*	9.3	1.9	10.7	2.7	4.50‡
PSLT Syntax	10.4	3.2	11.7	3.7	2.85†	9.0	2.2	11.7	3.6	6.67‡
PSLT Abstract-Concrete	12.6	3.9	13.9	3.6	2.67†	11.9	4.2	14.0	3.6	3.97‡
Metropolitan Spelling	9.6	1.4	10.7	1.3	5.81‡	8.8	1.3	10.6	1.2	9.48‡

IDENTIFICATION AND DIAGNOSIS

Metropolitan Language Arts	9.4	1.2	10.7	1.4	6.81‡	8.6	1.3	10.5	1.3	9.62‡
Arithmetic										
Metropolitan Arithmetic	9.2	0.6	9.7	0.8	4.79‡	9.0	0.9	10.2	1.0	8.49‡
PMA Arithmetic	9.4	0.9	10.3	1.1	5.69‡	8.9	0.7	9.7	0.8	7.87‡
Nonverbal										
Detroit Designs	9.8	1.8	10.7	1.9	3.87‡	9.0	1.8	10.6	1.8	6.90‡
Draw-A-Man	9.6	2.3	10.0	2.3	1.35	9.0	2.4	10.3	2.3	4.02‡
Healy I	11.2	2.4	12.2	2.7	3.19†	10.9	3.1	12.6	2.8	4.52‡
Leiter	9.0	1.2	9.9	1.5	4.41‡	8.6	1.2	9.9	1.4	6.67‡
Auditory Memory										
Detroit Words	7.9	2.3	9.2	2.4	4.19‡	8.0	2.2	9.2	2.6	3.64‡
Detroit Sentences	8.8	2.4	10.2	2.2	4.57‡	8.3	2.3	10.0	2.1	5.77‡
Detroit Oral Directions	9.9	2.1	11.0	2.1	4.15‡	9.5	2.1	11.1	2.1	5.13‡
Detroit Letters	10.0	1.5	11.0	1.9	4.45‡	9.6	1.4	10.9	1.8	6.24‡
Reading—Syllabication										
Wide-Range Oral Reading	10.2	1.8	11.9	2.4	6.07‡	9.0	1.3	11.6	2.2	10.89‡
Gates-McKillop Word Parts	10.2	1.3	11.2	0.9	6.64‡	9.3	1.5	11.2	1.0	11.68‡
Gates-McKillop Nonsense Words	9.6	0.9	10.2	0.6	5.41‡	8.9	1.0	10.1	0.6	10.43‡
Gates-McKillop Syllabication	9.7	1.4	10.9	0.9	7.51‡	8.7	1.3	10.8	1.0	13.23‡
Gates-Russell Oral Words	8.7	0.9	9.4	1.1	5.85‡	8.1	0.7	9.3	0.9	10.64‡
Gates-Russell One Syllable	9.4	2.0	10.8	2.0	5.14‡	8.6	1.7	10.6	2.0	7.98‡
Gates-Russell Two Syllables	9.4	1.8	10.7	1.6	5.69‡	8.5	1.6	10.6	1.6	9.54‡

*$p < 0.05$; †$p < 0.01$; ‡$p < 0.001$.

Table 3. Discriminant Analysis Results for 47 Test Scores for the Experimental Groups

Borderline	F	Learning Disability	F
Gates-McKillop Syllabication	51.45	Gates-McKillop Syllabication	111.53
Gates-MacGinitie Comprehension	33.50	Leiter	74.07
WISC Comprehension	24.43	Gates-MacGinitie Comprehension	53.91
PMA Arithmetic	19.44	WISC Comprehension	43.62
Gates-MacGinitie Accuracy	16.27	Healy I	37.05
WISC Similarities	14.00	Gates-McKillop Nonsense Words	32.76
Metropolitan Language	12.64	Gates-Russell 1 Syllable	29.49
Healy I	11.47	Gates-McKillop Word Parts	27.31
Draw-A-Man	10.59	PSLT Syntax	25.35
Detroit Letters	9.71	Mean Verbal M.A.	23.36
Detroit Sentences	9.00	Detroit Sentences	22.16
Gates-McKillop Nonsense Words	8.46	PMA Arithmetic	20.91
Metropolitan Spelling	7.95	WISC Coding	20.19
WISC Block Design	7.45	Mean Performance M.A.	19.12
Kent D	7.08	PSLT Total Words	18.27
Oral PSLT Words Per Sentence	6.71	Gates-Russell Oral Words	17.36
Oral PSLT Abstract-Concrete	6.38	Heath Rails	16.40
PSLT Abstract-Concrete	6.10	PSLT Total Sentences	15.49
Gates-McKillop Word Parts	5.83	Metropolitan Arithmetic	14.71
Gates-Russell 1 Syllable	5.57	Detroit Designs	13.99
Leiter	5.34	Detroit Verbal Opposites	13.35
Metropolitan Arithmetic	5.15	Gates-MacGinitie Accuracy	12.72
Detroit Free Association	4.96	Detroit Free Association	12.15
WISC Arithmetic	4.82	Oral PSLT Abstract-Concrete	11.63

IDENTIFICATION AND DIAGNOSIS

WISC Object Assembly	4.65	WISC Vocabulary	11.15
Detroit Orientation	4.48	Oral PSLT Words Per Sentence	10.70
PSLT Syntax	4.32	Detroit Oral Directions	10.30
Gates-Russell Oral Words	4.16	WISC Similarities	9.93
Detroit Verbal Opposites	4.03	Metropolitan Spelling	9.58
Gates-MacGinitie Vocabulary	3.90	Gates-Russell 2 Syllables	9.24
Heath Rails	3.76	Detroit Words	8.91
Detroit Oral Directions	3.63	Wide-Range Oral Reading	8.59
WISC Vocabulary	3.51	Detroit Orientation	8.28
PSLT Words Per Sentence	3.39	Metropolitan Language	7.99
Mean Performance M.A.	3.28	WISC Picture Completion	6.98
Vineland	3.17	WISC Information	6.76
Digit Span	3.07	PSLT Abstract-Concrete	6.54
WISC Picture Completion	2.97	WISC Digit Span	6.34
WISC Picture Arrangement	2.87	WISC Arithmetic	6.15
(Mean Performance M.A. is removed)	2.97	Kent D	5.97
WISC Coding	2.87	PSLT Words Per Sentence	5.79
PSLT Total Sentences	2.78	WISC Block Design	5.62
PSLT Total Words	2.70		
Mean Performance M.A.	2.62		
WISC Mazes	2.60		
Gates-Russell 2 Syllables	2.53		
Wide Range Oral Reading	2.46		

Not significant at 0.01: WISC Information
    Mean Verbal M.A.
    Detroit Words
    Detroit Designs

Not significant at 0.01: WISC Object Assembly
    WISC Mazes
    Vineland
    Draw-A-Man

functions for children who had poor success in school learning. This may be one of the most significant outcomes of this investigation, inasmuch as it has importance to definition and identification of learning-disability children. These children differ mainly in cognitive processing patterns. If further verified, results such as these may serve as the basis for development of a construct of the psychology of learning as it relates to children with this type of disability.

DISCRIMINANT ANALYSIS

A major objective was to evolve a psychoeducational test battery to assist in identifying learning-disability children. The discriminant analysis technique has proved useful in appraising tests for this purpose. The results for 47 of the test scores are shown in Table 3; all listed were significant at the 0.01 level or higher. Considerable agreement occurred, whether the learning disability was mild or severe. For both groups the most discriminating test was syllabication. This test requires that the child pronounce nonsense words that he sees. To perform well, he must recognize the letters and then convert them into their auditory equivalents; he must engage visual and auditory cognitive processes simultaneously. This facility seems critical to school learning. Other tests that discriminated between learning-deficit and normal children at a high level involved comprehension, ability to understand complex passages read to the child.

The discriminant analysis disclosed that a number of psychoeducational tests are effective in identifying learning-disability children, and in further clarifying the cognitive disturbances of these children. Hence, these tests are useful in making diagnoses and in planning for remedial education. The most critical cognitive disturbances are inability to associate verbal and nonverbal information and lack of facility in converting auditory information into visual, and visual into auditory.

OPHTHALMOLOGIC STUDY

The findings from the ophthalmologic study were analyzed in two ways: the general classification (normal–abnormal) and specific test findings. The results for the general classification are shown in Table 4. When the children's visual capacities were designated as normal (no defects), or as abnormal (defects present), there were no differences between the experimental and control groups. So far as these results are concerned, visual disorders did not contribute to the poor performance of the children having learning deficits.

To pursue further the role of visual defects, a statistical analysis was made of the incidence of each of the test findings. These results are presented in Table 5; the test of proportion was used to determine significance. The outcome of this analysis was revealing, because in no instance did any one of the ophthalmologic test items differentiate between the experimental and control groups. Although there were many children in the learning-deficient groups who were much below average in reading, in no instance was a given factor associated with this deficiency. No single abnormality of the visual mechanism was found to influence learning.

These negative findings were confirmed by other statistical analyses. The results were compared on the basis of type and degree of learning disability and, again, no relationships appeared. Finally, using the discriminant analysis technique, the groups were compared on the basis of the ophthalmologist's classifications of normal and abnormal. As in the case of the other statistical analyses, these data showed no association between visual defects and learning disabilities.

Table 4. Ophthalmologic Results When Categorized as Normal or Abnormal

Group	n	Normal	Abnormal	Proportion	χ^2
Borderline	112	91	21	0.80	
Control	112	95	17	0.84	0.51
				Difference −0.04	
Learning disability	108	91	17	0.84	
Control	108	95	13	0.86	0.62
				Difference −0.02	

Table 5. Findings of the Ophthalmologic Examination for the Borderline Group (n = 112) and Controls (n = 112), and for the Learning Disability Group (n = 108) and Controls (n = 108)

Specific Finding	Borderline	Control	Difference	Learning Disability	Control	Difference
Pupils equal	1.00	1.00	0.00	1.00	1.00	0.00
Pupil reaction to light						
Direct	1.00	1.00	0.00	1.00	1.00	0.00
Consensual	1.00	1.00	0.00	1.00	1.00	0.00
Mobility-versions	0.96	0.98	−0.02	0.97	0.99	−0.02
Corneal sensation	1.00	0.98	0.02	1.00	0.99	0.01
Convergence	0.92	0.92	0.00	0.91	0.92	−0.01
Visual fields	1.00	0.97	0.03	0.99	0.99	0.00
Color vision	0.96	0.95	0.01	0.95	0.94	0.01
Ocular fundi	1.00	1.00	0.00	0.99	1.00	0.01
Ocular Dominance	0.59	0.55	0.04	0.59	0.68	−0.08
Handedness	0.88	0.80	0.01	0.86	0.92	−0.06
Accommodation						
Right eye	0.99	0.98	0.01	0.98	0.98	0.00
Left eye	0.98	0.98	0.00	0.97	0.97	0.00
Vision Unaided Distance						
Right eye	0.93	0.96	−0.03	0.93	0.94	−0.01
Left eye	0.93	0.96	−0.03	0.93	0.94	−0.01
Vision unaided Near						
Right eye	0.96	1.00	−0.04	0.98	0.99	−0.01
Left eye	0.96	1.00	−0.04	0.98	0.99	0.01

Table 6. Results of EEG Classifications for the Experimental and Control Groups

Group	n	Abnormal	Normal	Proportion	χ^2
Borderline	101	48	53	0.52	
Control	101	32	69	0.68	5.22*
				Difference 0.16*	
Learning disability	99	35	64	0.65	
Control	99	26	73	0.73	2.94
				Difference −0.08	

*$p < 0.05$.

ELECTROENCEPHALOGRAPHIC STUDY

A number of learning-disability children present problems of distractibility, hyperactivity, and seizure proneness. Moreover, electroencephalographic findings are associated with behavior disorders, especially as these relate to various types of learning deficits. In previous investigations, EEG results revealed the critical manner in which electrocortical disturbances and poor school performance might be related, and the importance of such associations to program planning.[2]

An intensive electroencephalographic study was made of the children, experimental and control; this was unusual in that it permitted comparison of normal and learning-disability children of the same sex and age, with the pairs being selected from the same classroom. As in the other areas studied, the EEG investigator was unaware of the child's classification at the time of reading the record. The electroencephalographer provided two types of data: classification as normal or abnormal and a detailed record of the objective findings. Both types of information were analyzed statistically.

The results of the general classifications for the experimental and control groups are given in Table 6. There were no significant differences between the learning-disability and control groups, whereas there were more abnormal EEGs for the borderline group as compared to the normal. The EEG findings were negative for the more involved sample, but positive for those with slight deficits in learning. Hughes[3] has presented a detailed discussion of these results. The objective findings also were coded and analyzed statistically (see Table 7). The results for the learning disability sample again were negative. One significant finding appearing in the borderline group was the occurrence of more focal slow waves in these children.

Consideration was given to the possibility that type and degree of involvement might be a factor in EEG dysfunctions, especially in view of the positive findings for those with borderline deficits in learning. Using the general classifications (normal–abnormal), an analysis was made by group, holding these variables constant (see Table 8). The subjects were ranked by LQ scores according to three types of disability: reading, nonverbal, and mixed. The learning disability and borderline children who were deficient only in reading, those deficient only in nonverbal functions, and those deficient in a combination of these facets of learning were compared with their respective controls. This analysis disclosed that children classified psychologically as being deficient in nonverbal learning had more abnormal EEGs; no differences appeared for the poor reading and mixed groups.

To summarize, relationships between electrocortical abnormalities and learning disabilities appeared only for children with slight or moderate deficits. Focal slow waves more often characterized this group. According to Hughes,[3] those with slight deficits were reacting more and, hence, were less deficient. The more severely involved group showed less reactivity and, therefore, greater deficits in learning.

Children with nonverbal disturbances of learning had abnormal EEGs much more often than poor readers or those with mixed disorders; the type of involvement was a significant factor. It might be that when involvement occurs on the right hemisphere (the hemisphere mainly responsible for nonverbal aspects of learning), there is a greater possibility of electrocortical dysfunctioning.

Although few characteristic patterns emerged, children with deficits in learning showed evidence of brain dysfunction. Inasmuch as the experimental sample was selected only on the basis of discrepancy between expected and actual learning achieve-

Table 7. EEG Objective Findings for Borderline Group ($n = 101$) and Controls ($n = 101$) and for the Learning Disability Group ($n = 99$) and Controls ($n = 99$)

Findings	Borderline	Control	Difference	Learning Disability	Control	Difference
Slow waves						
Diffuse	0.96	0.97	−0.01	0.95	0.96	−0.01
Focal	0.75	0.89	−0.14*	0.87	0.88	−0.01
Sharp waves						
Diffuse	1.00	1.00	0.00	1.00	1.00	0.00
Focal	0.96	0.94	0.02	0.95	0.95	0.00
Sharp waves (Centrencephalic)						
Under 3/sec	1.00	1.00	0.00	1.00	0.99	0.01
3/sec	0.98	0.99	−0.01	0.99	0.99	0.00
6/sec	1.00	0.99	0.01	1.00	0.98	0.02
Positive spikes	0.74	0.83	−0.09	0.86	0.85	0.01
Depression						
Diffuse	0.98	0.99	−0.01	0.99	0.99	0.00
Focal	1.00	1.00	0.00	1.00	1.00	0.00
Excessive						
Fast waves	0.98	0.97	0.01	0.96	0.98	−0.02
Background rhythm	0.50	0.48	0.01	0.52	0.48	0.03
Hyperventilation	0.97	1.00	−0.03	1.00	0.99	0.01
Photic driving	0.52	0.61	−0.09	0.56	0.64	−0.08

*$p < 0.05$.

Table 8. EEG Results by Type and Degree of Disorder in Learning

Type of Disability	n	LQ Range	Borderline Abnormal	Borderline Normal	Control Abnormal	Control Normal	χ^2
Reading	19	85–89	10	9	8	11	0.42
Nonverbal	18	85–89	8	10	1	17	7.26*
Mixed	64	85–89	30	34	23	41	0.93
Total	101		48	53	32	69	
			Learning Disability Abnormal	Learning Disability Normal	Control Abnormal	Control Normal	
Reading	33	72–84	12	21	9	24	0.63
Nonverbal	20	65–84	6	14	6	14	0.00
Mixed	46	71–84	17	29	11	35	1.85
Total	99		35	64	26	73	

*$p < 0.01$.

Table 9. Neurologic Examination Results When Categorized as Normal or Abnormal

Group	n	Classification Normal	Classification Abnormal	Proportion of Normalcy	χ^2
Borderline	104	55	49	0.53	1.97
Control	104	65	39	0.63	
				Difference −0.10	
Learning disability	99	49	50	0.50	2.94
Control	99	61	38	0.63	
				Difference −0.13	

Table 10. Individual Neurologic Findings for the Borderline Group (n = 104) and Controls (n = 104) and for the Learning Disability Group (n = 99) and Controls (n = 99)*

Sign	Borderline	Control	Difference	Learning Disability	Control	Difference
Gait: rate of progression	1.00	0.97	0.03	0.99	0.99	0.00
Base	0.99	0.98	0.01	1.00	0.99	0.01
Right bicep jerk	0.84	0.81	0.03	0.85	0.82	0.03
Left bicep jerk	0.83	0.81	0.02	0.85	0.82	0.03
Right tricep jerk	0.88	0.86	0.02	0.91	0.86	0.05
Left tricep jerk	0.88	0.86	0.02	0.91	0.86	0.05
Right waist jerk	0.83	0.82	0.01	0.84	0.84	0.00
Left waist jerk	0.82	0.82	0.00	0.84	0.84	0.00
Right ulnar jerk	0.78	0.78	0.00	0.80	0.80	0.00
Left ulnar jerk	0.77	0.78	-0.02	0.80	0.80	0.00
Jaw jerk	1.00	0.98	0.02	1.00	0.97	0.03
Right knee jerk	0.92	0.94	-0.02	0.95	0.95	0.00
Left knee jerk	0.92	0.93	-0.01	0.92	0.94	-0.02
Right ankle jerk	0.96	0.91	-0.05	0.99	0.96	0.03
Left ankle jerk	0.95	0.91	0.04	0.97	0.96	0.01
Right Hoffman maneuver	1.00	1.00	0.00	1.00	1.00	0.00
Left Hoffman maneuver	1.00	1.00	0.00	1.00	1.00	0.00
Snouting	0.98	1.00	-0.02	0.98	1.00	-0.02
Sucking	1.00	1.00	0.00	1.00	1.00	0.00
Right palmomental	0.92	0.95	-0.03	0.95	0.99	-0.04
Left palmomental	0.90	0.95	-0.05	0.95	1.00	-0.05
Right clonus	0.97	0.99	-0.02	0.98	0.97	0.01
Left clonus	0.96	0.98	-0.02	0.98	0.96	0.02
Right Plantar B	0.94	0.97	-0.03	0.94	0.96	-0.02
Left Plantar B	0.92	0.96	-0.04	0.95	0.96	-0.01
Right Plantar C	1.00	0.99	0.01	1.00	0.99	0.01
Left Plantar C	1.00	0.99	0.01	0.99	0.99	0.00
Right Oppenheim	1.00	1.00	0.00	1.00	1.00	0.00
Left Oppenheim	1.00	1.00	0.00	0.99	1.00	-0.01
Right superficial abdominal	0.98	0.98	0.00	0.97	0.99	-0.02
Left superficial abdominal	0.98	0.98	0.00	0.98	0.98	0.00
Right Plantar G†	1.00	1.00	0.00	1.00	1.00	0.00
Left Plantar G†	1.00	1.00	0.00	1.00	1.00	0.00
Right Cremaster‡	0.92	0.97	-0.04	0.88	0.94	-0.05

IDENTIFICATION AND DIAGNOSIS

Left Cremaster‡	0.94	0.97	-0.03	0.90	0.92	-0.03
Right pupillary	1.00	1.00	0.00	1.00	1.00	0.00
Left pupillary	1.00	1.00	0.00	1.00	1.00	0.00
Right light	1.00	1.00	0.00	1.00	1.00	0.00
Left light	1.00	1.00	0.00	1.00	1.00	0.00
Right accommodation	1.00	1.00	0.00	1.00	1.00	0.00
Left accommodation	1.00	1.00	0.00	1.00	1.00	0.00
Right consensual	1.00	1.00	0.00	1.00	1.00	0.00
Left consensual	1.00	1.00	0.00	1.00	1.00	0.00
Right pharyngeal	0.99	1.00	0.00	1.00	1.00	0.00
Left pharyngeal	0.99	1.00	0.00	1.00	1.00	0.00
Right pilomotor	1.00	1.00	0.00	1.00	1.00	0.00
Left pilomotor	1.00	1.00	0.00	1.00	1.00	0.00
Right vasomotor	1.00	0.99	0.01	1.00	1.00	0.00
Left vasomotor	1.00	0.99	0.01	1.00	1.00	0.00
Right pin prick	1.00	1.00	0.00	1.00	1.00	0.00
Left pin prick	1.00	1.00	0.00	1.00	1.00	0.00
Right cotton touch	1.00	1.00	0.00	1.00	1.00	0.00
Left cotton touch	1.00	1.00	0.00	1.00	1.00	0.00
Right temperature	1.00	1.00	0.00	1.00	1.00	0.00
Left temperature	1.00	1.00	0.00	1.00	1.00	0.00
Right vibration	1.00	1.00	0.00	1.00	1.00	0.00
Left vibration	1.00	1.00	0.00	1.00	1.00	0.00
Right position	1.00	1.00	0.00	1.00	1.00	0.00
Left position	1.00	1.00	0.00	1.00	1.00	0.00
Right stereognosis	0.88	0.88	0.01	0.86	0.89	-0.03
Left stereognosis	0.89	0.88	0.01	0.86	0.89	-0.03
Right barognosis	0.96	0.99	-0.03	0.97	0.96	0.01
Left barognosis	0.96	0.99	-0.03	0.97	0.96	0.01
Right two point discrimination	0.96	1.00	-0.04	0.99	1.00	-0.01
Left two point discrimination	0.96	1.00	-0.04	0.99	1.00	-0.01
Right skin writing	0.65	0.80	0.14*	0.76	0.80	-0.04
Left skin writing	0.65	0.80	0.14*	0.78	0.80	-0.02
Right extinction to DDS	0.86	0.88	-0.01	0.86	0.87	-0.01
Left extinction to DDS	0.86	0.88	-0.01	0.86	0.87	-0.01
Right touch localization-Bilateral	0.86	0.97	-0.11	0.90	0.95	-0.05
Left touch localization-Bilateral	0.85	0.97	-0.12	0.90	0.95	-0.05
Smell	0.90	0.96	-0.06	0.92	0.97	-0.05
Right vision	1.00	1.00	0.00	1.00	1.00	0.00

(Continued)

Table 10. Individual Neurologic Findings for the Borderline Group (n = 104) and Controls (n = 104) and for the Learning Disability Group (n = 99) and Controls (n = 99) (Cont'd)

Sign	Borderline	Control	Difference	Learning Disability	Control	Difference
Left vision	1.00	1.00	0.00	1.00	1.00	0.00
Fundi	1.00	1.00	0.00	1.00	1.00	0.00
Right opticokinetic nystagmus	0.95	0.93	0.02	0.95	0.95	0.00
Left opticokinetic nystagmus	0.94	0.93	0.01	0.96	0.95	0.01
Right jaw movement—vertical	0.99	0.97	0.02	0.98	0.99	−0.01
Left jaw movement—vertical	0.99	0.97	0.02	0.98	0.99	−0.01
Right facial movement	0.97	0.97	0.00	0.96	0.99	−0.03
Left facial movement	0.98	0.97	0.01	0.99	0.99	0.00
Right taste	0.89	0.97	−0.09	0.98	0.97	0.01
Left taste	0.89	0.97	−0.08	0.98	0.97	0.01
Right hearing	0.99	1.00	−0.01	0.98	0.98	0.00
Left hearing	0.99	0.99	0.00	0.98	0.97	0.01
Equilibrium	1.00	1.00	0.00	1.00	1.00	0.00
Right motion: palate–pharynx	0.98	0.98	0.00	1.00	0.99	0.01
Left motion: palate–pharynx	0.98	0.98	0.00	1.00	0.99	0.01
Right motion: trapezius	1.00	1.00	0.00	1.00	1.00	0.00
Left motion: trapezius	1.00	1.00	0.00	0.99	1.00	−0.01
Tongue protrusion	0.99	0.99	0.00	0.99	1.00	−0.01
Tongue—vertical	0.99	0.92	0.01	0.84	0.95	−0.11
Right index to thumb	0.96	0.98	−0.02	0.97	0.99	−0.02
Left index to thumb	0.95	0.97	−0.02	0.96	0.99	−0.03
Right pronation—supination	0.89	0.88	0.01	0.89	0.91	−0.02
Left pronation—supination	0.89	0.88	0.01	0.89	0.91	−0.02
Right finger–finger–nose	1.00	1.00	0.00	1.00	1.00	0.00
Left finger–finger–nose	1.00	1.00	0.00	0.99	1.00	−0.01
Right cheek reflexes	1.00	1.00	0.00	1.00	1.00	0.00
Left cheek reflexes	1.00	1.00	0.00	1.00	1.00	0.00
Right past-point	0.99	1.00	−0.01	0.99	1.00	−0.01
Left past-point	0.99	1.00	−0.01	0.99	1.00	−0.01
Right metria	1.00	1.00	0.00	1.00	1.00	0.00
Left metria	1.00	1.00	0.00	1.00	1.00	0.00
Associative movements with multiple postural acts at 10 sec	0.74	0.78	−0.04	0.67	0.79	−0.12
Right touch localization—unilateral	0.99	0.98	0.01	1.00	0.99	0.01

Left touch localization—unilateral	0.99	0.98	0.01	1.00	0.01
Right visual fields	1.00	1.00	0.00	1.00	0.00
Left visual fields	1.00	1.00	0.00	1.00	0.00
Jaw movement—lateral	0.87*	0.89	0.03	0.85	-0.04
Tongue alternating movement—horizontal	0.77	0.82	0.05	0.69	-0.11
Right drumming†	0.96	0.97	-0.01	0.94	-0.01
Left drumming†	0.96	0.97	-0.01	0.95	-0.04
Right heel-to-shin†	1.00	0.99	0.01	0.99	0.01
Left heel-to-shin†	1.00	0.97	0.03	0.99	0.01
Right gait: swinging arms†	1.00	1.00	0.00	1.00	0.00
Left gait: swinging arms†	1.00	1.00	0.00	1.00	0.00
Tandem walking	0.86	0.86	0.00	0.82	-0.03
Right standing on one foot†	0.90	0.90	0.00	0.83	-0.09
Left standing on one foot†	0.87	0.90	-0.03	0.81	-0.12
Right hopping on one foot†	0.92	0.94	-0.01	0.95	0.02
Left hopping on one foot†	0.92	0.94	-0.01	0.92	-0.01
Romberg†	1.00	1.00	0.00	1.00	0.00
Hand-to-nose, hand-to-ear†	0.67	0.78	-0.11	0.72	-0.03
Grip hands: fingers facing tip-to-tip†	0.91	0.92	-0.01	0.91	0.00
Pat stomach—rub head†	0.86	0.92	-0.06	0.91	0.00
Associative movements with multiple postural act 20"†	0.73	0.78	-0.05	0.65	-0.13
Involuntary movements: specific†	1.00	0.99	0.01	0.99	0.00
Right muscle tone: arm†	1.00	1.00	0.00	1.00	0.00
Left muscle tone: arm†	1.00	1.00	0.00	1.00	0.00
Right muscle tone: leg†	1.00	1.00	0.00	1.00	0.00
Left muscle tone: leg†	1.00	0.99	0.01	1.00	0.00
Right muscle strength: arm†	1.00	1.00	0.00	1.00	0.00
Left muscle strength: arm†	1.00	1.00	0.00	1.00	0.00
Right muscle strength: legs†	1.00	1.00	0.00	1.00	0.00
Left muscle strength: legs†	1.00	1.00	0.00	1.00	0.00
Power: trunk†	1.00	1.00	0.00	1.00	0.00

*$p < 0.05$.
†Proportions based on 79 borderlines and 79 controls.
‡Proportions based on 78 learning disabilities and 78 controls.

ment (not by clinical, disease entities), these data suggest the importance of the EEG in identification, diagnosis, and treatment of this type of handicapped child.

PEDIATRIC NEUROLOGIC STUDY

The pediatric neurologist conducted a physical examination of each subject, experimental and control, without awareness of the child's classification; these data were analyzed statistically using the test of proportions. No significant differences appeared. The total population, with or without deficits in learning, was in good physical condition.

As with the other medical data, the neurologic findings were analyzed in two primary ways: general classification of normal–abnormal and objective test results. The comparisons by overall classification are shown in Table 9. There was a trend for the children with deficits in learning to be classified more often as abnormal, but the difference was not statistically significant.

The groups also were compared on each individual test, a total of 137 signs (see Table 10). The only statistically significant differences were for skin writing, with the borderline children showing more positive signs than the controls. No severe neurologic dysfunctions were found, but it must be noted that children with obvious motor disorders were eliminated from the sample.

Other analyses of the neurologist's findings involved comparison by incidence of positive signs (see Table 11). Many more abnormal neurologic signs appeared in the children with learning deficits. When the number of positive signs served as the parameter, the learning-disability children presented a far greater incidence of actual neurologic disturbances. This was true also of the suspect signs. When the borderline and learning disability groups were compared by degree of neurologic involvement, more

Table 11. Incidence of Abnormal and Suspect Neurologic Signs by Group

	Abnormal Signs	Proportion	Z	Suspect Signs	Proportion	Z
Borderline	106	0.77	14.94*	576	0.52	3.09†
Control	32	0.23		525	0.48	
Total	138	1.00		1101	1.00	
Learning disability	93	0.73	11.82*	528	0.53	3.36*
Control	34	0.27		475	0.47	
Total	127	1.00		1003	1.00	

*$p < 0.001$.
†$p < 0.01$.

Table 12. Incidence of Abnormal and Suspect Neurologic Signs for Learning Disability and Borderline Groups

	Abnormal Signs	Proportion	Z
Learning disability	93	0.47	−1.85
Borderline	106	0.53	
Total	199	1.00	
	Suspect Signs		
Learning disability	528	0.48	−2.89*
Borderline	576	0.52	
Total	1104	1.00	

*$p < 0.01$.

suspect signs appeared for the borderline children (see Table 12); when the deficit in learning was minimal, the most common neurologic signs also were minimal.

In review, there has been speculation regarding the role of neurology in the identification and diagnosis of children with learning disabilities. The results from this investigation reveal that the neurologist can contribute significant data, even when given the complex task of distinguishing between good and poor learners. Nevertheless, characteristic patterns of neurologic involvement did not emerge, although as with the EEG, those with nonverbal disturbances showed a higher incidence of positive neurologic signs. The validity of the neurologist's findings is supported in that the borderline group manifested more soft signs, whereas the learning-disability children showed more of the hard signs.

If the sample of children with learning deficiencies had been selected by clinical criteria (i.e., positive birth history, hyperactivity, seizure status) more patterns of neurologic dysfunction might have occurred. Therefore, in view of the stringencies applied by the research paradigm, the results suggest a relationship between neurologic disturbance and deficiencies in learning. Neurologic studies can be helpful in identification, diagnosis, and treatment of learning-disability children.

ACKNOWLEDGMENT

The collaboration of the research team is gratefully acknowledged: Benjamin Boshes, co-director; John R. Hughes, electroencephalographer; Lawrence J. Lawson, ophthalmologist; Dragomir M. Vuckovich, pediatric neurologist; Naomi K. Zigmond and Don A. Olson, coordinators; Otis D. Turner, project officer. Appreciation is expressed to the consultants, research associates, parents, children, and schools involved.

REFERENCES

1. Clements, S.: Minimal Brain Dysfunction: Terminology and Identification. NINDB Monograph No. 3, PHS, No. 1415. Washington, D.C., U.S. Department of Health, Education and Welfare, 1966.

2. Hughes, J.: Electroencephalography and learning. In Myklebust, H. (Ed.): Progress in Learning Disabilities, Vol. I. New York, Grune & Stratton, 1968, p. 113.

3. —: Electroencephalography and learning disabilities. In Myklebust, H. (Ed.): Progress in Learning Disabilities, Vol. II. New York, Grune & Stratton, 1971, p. 18.

4. Killen, J.: Relationships between psychodynamic factors and nonverbal cognitive processes in normal and learning-disability children. Unpublished dissertation. DeKalb, Ill., Northern Illinois University, 1972.

5. Myklebust, H.: Learning disabilities: Definition and overview. In Myklebust, H. (Ed.): Progress in Learning Disabilities, Vol. I. New York, Grune & Stratton, 1968, p. 1.

6. —, Killen, J., and Bannochie, M.: Learning disabilities and cognitive processes. In Myklebust, H. (Ed.): Progress in Learning Disabilities, Vol. II. New York, Grune & Stratton, 1971, p. 213.

Neurologic and Behavioral Assessment of Children With Minimal Brain Dysfunction

B. C. L. Touwen, M.D., and A. F. Kalverboer, Ph.D.

In the first part of this article, some basic requirements for the neurologic assessment of children with minimal brain dysfunction (MBD) are formulated. The neurologic tests must reflect neural mechanisms. The examination must be age-specific, standardized for technique and data recording, and the behavioral state of the child must be accounted for throughout the examination. The difficulties of interpretation and diagnosis are discussed. A neurologic profile is presented as a means for the quantification of the results. In the second part, the method of observation and quantitative analysis of "free-field" behavior is discussed with particular reference to the MBD problem. How insight into the child's maladaptive behavior can be gained by systematically varying the environment is pointed out. Important variables are novelty vs. familiarity of the environment, presence vs. absence of social figure(s), and presence vs. absence of additional material(s). Subsequently, limiting factors in designing observational studies and some problems concerning the choice of behavioral categories are discussed. The method of free-field observation is particularly applicable to the study of behavioral characteristics, such as hyperactivity and attentional disorders, which are often observed in MBD children.

TERMS SUCH AS "minimal brain dysfunction" are used to identify children in the normal range of intelligence who show patterns of behavior and learning disorders that are assumed to be related to "minimal" dysfunction of the nervous system.

A review of the extensive literature on the MBD syndrome shows that descriptions of the syndrome vary considerably. Similarly, opinions as to the etiology have vacillated between considering this syndrome to be entirely organic, or entirely environmental and psychogenic, or some combination of the two. Rutter's conclusion "that there is no 'one brain damage syndrome' but rather many different psychiatric disorders resulting from interaction between neurological dysfunction, family disturbance and social circumstance"[25] would, therefore, seem justified. Most clinicians recognize that the term "minimal brain dysfunction" has little meaning except as a descriptive eponym, and they would probably agree with Eisenberg: "What is at stake is our ability to recognize and differentiate clinical syndromes, the specification of which will be necessary for effective research on causes and for meaningful attempts to evaluate treatment."[6]

In order to achieve such aims, it will be necessary to refine our current techniques of observation and analysis.

In this report, we will discuss a standardized method of neurologic examination for detecting signs of minor nervous dysfunction, and an approach to the observation of

---

The follow-up studies on which this paper is based were supported by a grant from the Organization for Health Research T.N.O. (The Netherlands).

Reprint requests should be addressed to B. C. L. Touwen, M.D., Department of Developmental Neurology, University Hospital, Oostersingel 59/Groningen, The Netherlands.

behavior in a "free-field" setting. The methods described may provide insights into the complex etiologic, diagnostic, and therapeutic problems presented by MBD children.

I. THE NEUROLOGIC ASSESSMENT OF MBD CHILDREN

Strategy of Examination Technique

The essential aspects for the design of any neurologic assessment must include the selection of the tests, which should be age-specific and representative for the neural functions to be assessed; the standardization of the technique; the standardization of the behavioral state; the quantitative recording of the results; and, finally, the sequence in which the assessment should be carried out. Such a formalization of the design has been offered by Prechtl.[21,22]

Test Selection: Age specificity of tests. The neurologic examination of the child must differ qualitatively from that of the adult because the nervous system of the two is qualitatively different. The dynamic properties of the child's nervous system stand in striking contrast to the relatively static phase of development of the adult organism. The examination technique must, therefore, be age-specific.

Age specificity has two aspects. First, the results of the examination for any specific nervous function will vary according to the age. We must know the manifestations of the different subsystems of the nervous system at consecutive ages. Since the development of neurologic functions is a continuous process with large individual variations in rate, it is often difficult, if not impossible, to identify well-circumscribed and qualitatively distinct developmental stages. This has been shown for some motor phenomena in infancy,[16,26] and there is no reason to assume that it is not also the case in later childhood.

Second, the strategy of the neurologic examination will depend largely on the age of the child and on his stage of development. Many of the so-called "primitive infantile responses" will have disappeared long before school age (e.g., the Moro response and rooting) and need not be tested. At the same time one must use different techniques for testing motor coordination in 3- and 10-yr-old children.

Test Selection: Representative tests. The main criteria in the selection of tests for a neurologic examination are that the assessment be comprehensive, and the results be directly referable to neural mechanisms. The latter criterion is often overlooked in textbooks for the neurologic examination of children,[12,17,19] so that tests are included whose relationship to neural mechanisms is unknown. Especially in the examination of children who present primarily with behavioral symptoms and learning disorders, it may be confusing to include tests that are meant to evaluate specific neural mechanisms, but at the same time involve behavioral characteristics which cannot be related directly to known neural mechanisms. In our selection we have tried, therefore, to avoid such tests.

The neural functions to be assessed can be subdivided according to the subsystems of the nervous system, including posture, sensorimotor apparatus, motility, coordination of trunk and extremities, fine manual and finger manipulations, and sensory functions such as the visual system. Employing the foregoing criteria, representative neurologic test items can be selected for these subsystems.

Associated movements (co-movements, synkinesias) have been emphasized by various authors as useful for identifying the relative maturation of the nervous system.[1,5,7,29] In our experience, their intercorrelation and association with other neurologic signs are relatively weak in preschool children (Touwen, unpublished data).

However, they may be helpful in assessing maturational delay in older children and are, therefore, included in the examination procedure.

Other aspects of behavior, such as activity level, concentration, and attention span, cannot be regarded as neurologic phenomena, since they cannot be related directly to known neural mechanisms. Tests that evaluate such functions, therefore, do not belong to a neurologic assessment. Neither do test procedures whose results are open to several interpretations—for example, sorting tasks or Oseretsky-type tests whose results may be strongly influenced by intelligence level, verbal potential, motivation, and social maturity. Tests that measure phenomena whose neural mechanisms are poorly understood, such as the "imitation of gestures,"[2] also are not suitable for inclusion in the neurologic examination.

The functions of hearing and vision meet the stipulated criteria only in part since the results of routine hearing and vision tests are multiconditioned and may be difficult to interpret. A screening of these functions may be included in the neurologic examination, but the results should be analyzed separately. The same applies to the assessment of speech development.

In our opinion, the results of tests for sensory functions such as stereognosis, two-point discrimination, tactile stimulation, and pain are very unreliable in childhood, especially in the case of children with behavioral disorders. Since they are usually highly intercorrelated with other neurologic abnormalities, tests for these functions may be omitted from the neurologic examination.

Standardization: Behavioral state. The control for the behavioral state of the child during the examination is an important part of the standardization of the procedure.[20] Unless the behavioral state is taken into account, a quantification of almost no finding is meaningful.

In the newborn, behavioral state can be classified according to whether the infant is asleep (regular or irregular sleep) or awake (quiet, active or crying).[23] Older infants and children will always be awake during the neurologic examination but they, too, may be quiet, fussing or crying, and this aspect of the behavioral state may considerably influence the results of testing (for instance, the resistance to passive moments or the evaluation of reflex thresholds). However, another aspect of behavioral state is important in these older infants and children. This aspect can be described in terms of social responsiveness (degree of interest, reluctance, refusal to fulfill demands), the level of which will not only influence the results of tests such as those for coordination or gross motor functioning (walking, walking on heels, on tiptoe, standing on one leg, hopping), but will also decide the reliability of the whole examination.

It is evident that the two aspects of behavioral state show considerable overlap. Nevertheless, it is useful to distinguish them, since fussing or crying, for instance, need not inevitably lead to reluctance or refusal; nor will a child who refuses to fulfill demands always cry. For a reliable interpretation of the results of the neurologic assessment, it is therefore necessary to record changes in both aspects of the behavioral state during the course of the examination.

Standardization: Technique.[28] The reliable detection of minor nervous dysfunctions depends on the use of strictly standardized methods of examination. Techniques for the elicitation of responses must be standardized. The responses should be recorded in a quantitative, descriptive way, so as to avoid subjective interpretations.

The sequence in which the tests are carried out should also be standardized and should be arranged to ensure that the child's cooperation is maintained. The most disruptive parts of the examination, like those that require total undressing, or lying down, and the examination of the head, should be postponed to the end.

Some parts of the examination are more fatiguing than others, and fatigue will influence test results. Thus, the results of tests for fine manipulative abilities may be different when the tests are carried out before or after hopping 20 times on each foot.

Finally, the external conditions during the examination should also be standardized as much as possible, since variables such as light, temperature, objects in the doctor's office (medical paraphernalia), and the examiner's clothes (white coat) may influence the child's social responsiveness.

Interpretation and Diagnosis

The interpretation of the neurologic findings is often complicated; only a complete examination provides the basis for a valid interpretation. Sometimes the findings can be arranged in a pattern that is recognizable from the point of view of clinical neurology; often, however, the findings do not fit into a clear pattern, or they are so slight that their significance or reliability is in doubt. Such findings are often called "soft signs," in contrast to "hard signs," whose significance and reliability should be evident.

Rutter et al. have discussed extensively the problem of soft vs. hard signs.[25] They concluded that the "softness" of many soft signs is related to issues of interpretation rather than of reliability, and that many a "hard" sign is far less reliable than is usually assumed. The authors have proposed that the terms "soft" and "hard" should be discarded.

In our view, a neurologic finding should at the very least fulfill the criterion of reliable elicitation. Only then can the significance, which may vary from individual to individual and depends on the association with other findings, be assessed. With very few exceptions (such as papilledema), no neurologic sign has meaning when found in isolation.

Still, a set of reliably elicited findings that does not permit a clear-cut neurologic diagnosis may be present, particularly in children with MBD. Our approach in such cases is to construct a descriptive neurologic profile of the child.

The Neurologic Profile

As mentioned previously, it is possible to arrange the items of the neurologic examination into groups that test hypothetical subsystems of the nervous system. Such groups of items account for posture, sensorimotor apparatus, body balance, coordination, fine manipulative ability, gross motor functions, quality of motility, and visual system. For practical reasons, associated movements and the presence or absence of dyskinesias (such as choreiform movements) can be recorded as separate categories of findings. On theoretical, empirical, and clinical grounds, age-specific population norms can be established for each item of the groups. The number of items fulfilling the norms can be counted separately for each group, and so a profile can be drawn (Table 1; Fig. 1).

Such a profile is purely descriptive. The yes or no fashion in which each item is recorded on the profile gives a quantification of nervous integrity in terms of the hypothesized subsystems of the nervous system. However, such a descriptive profile can be interpreted only when evaluated in combination with the raw data. When the data of the complete examination are available, the specific item that falls outside the normative value can be traced immediately. The justification for deriving a quantitative

Table 1. Groups of Items for the Theoretical Subsystems of the Nervous System*

(1) Sensorimotor Apparatus	(6) (Dys)kinesia
Resistance to passive movement	Choreiform movements arms and hands
Muscle power	Choreiform movements trunk and face
Range of movements	Athetotiform movements
Muscle consistency	Tremor
Knee jerk	(7) Gross Motor Functions
Ankle jerk	Heel-toe gait during walking
Threshold muscle reflexes legs	Walking on tiptoe
Biceps reflex	Walking on heels
Triceps reflex	Standing on one leg
Threshold muscle reflexes arms	Hopping on one leg
Abnominal skin reflex	Rising into sitting from supine position
Footsole reflex	(8) Quality of motility
Other exteroceptive reflexes big toe	Speed ⎫
(2) Posture	Smoothness ⎬ Small motor movements
Sitting, general	Adequacy ⎭
Feet, sitting	Speed ⎫
Standing, general	Smoothness ⎬ Gross motor movements
Legs, standing	Adequacy ⎭
Feet, standing	(9) Associated Movements
Extended arms, standing	Mouth-opening-finger-spreading phe-
Walking	nomenon
Lying in prone and supine position	A.M. accompanying diadochokinesis in
(3) Balance of Trunk	opposite hand
Response to push, standing	A.M. accompanying walking on tiptoe
Following object with eyes and head	A.M. accompanying walking on heels
Romberg	A.M. accompanying index-thumb grasp
Rebound phenomenon	(10) Visual System
Walking along a straight line	Position of the eyes
(4) Coordination of the Extremities	Directional nystagmus
Finger tip nose test	Position nystagmus
Diadochokinesis	Optokinetic nystagmus
Knee-heel test	Pursuit movements of the eyes
Kicking against examiner's hand	Visual fields
Finger-tip touching test	Fundoscopy
(5) Fine Manipulative Ability	
Finger-opposition test	
Follow-a-finger test	
Circle-test	

*For the technique and scoring of the items see the report by Touwen and Prechtl.[28]

score for the integrity of the nervous system is based on the assumption that the number of abnormal signs will increase in proportion to the intensity and the extent of the cerebral dysfunction.

The advantage of the profile is twofold. First, it provides a method for data reduction. Second, it enables the examiner to evaluate the degree of integrity of the nervous system in differential terms. It may be argued that the scores on the profile will be highly intercorrelated. Data from a group of 5-yr-old children, however, show that the correlation coefficient among subsystems describing sensorimotor, coordination, kinetic, and visual functions does not exceed 0.28 ($n = 169$).[27]

Such a profile is no substitute for the comprehensive neurologic assessment. Understandably, there is great demand for a short neurologic screening method that will

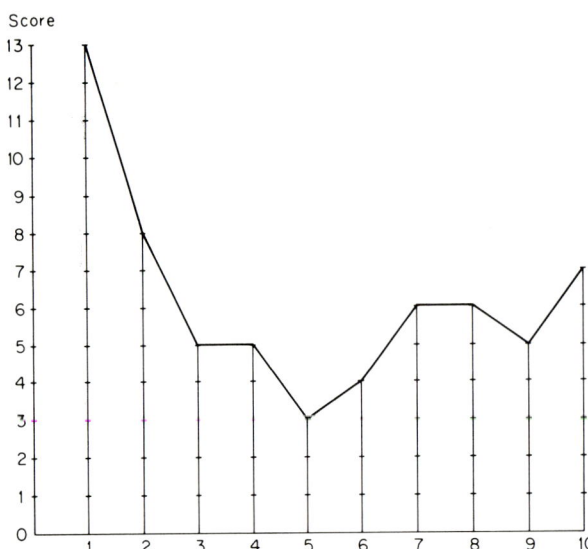

Fig. 1. A profile of the integrity of the nervous system, differentiated in 10 subsystems, which are numbered horizontally on the graph. With the number of test items given in parentheses, the subsystems are: 1, sensorimotor apparatus (13); 2, posture (8); 3, balance of trunk (5); 4, coordination of the extremities (5); 5, fine manipulative ability (3); 6, (dys)kinesia (4); 7, gross motor functions (6); 8, quality of motility (6); 9, associated movements (5); and 10, visual system (7). The number of items that are performed correctly is scored vertically for each subsystem. The drawn profile represents the highest possible score.

permit a rapid assessment of the integrity of the central nervous system. The complexity of the nervous system, however, makes it impossible to construct a screening device that will, at the same time, give reliable results. At the present time, it is impossible to identify one or two "crucial" neurologic tests that will reveal whether the brain is functioning normally or abnormally. Whether it will be possible to do so in the future seems doubtful.

Conclusion

The relationship between behavioral disorders and disturbed brain mechanisms can only be analyzed if both can be assessed quantitatively.

The neurologic assessment, discussed in the foregoing paragraphs, is one contribution to the analysis of brain mechanisms. Other tools, such as EEG recording, are dealt with in other chapters in this volume.

The behavioral aspects of the MBD syndrome, which also require careful operational definition and quantification, are discussed in the second part of this paper.

II. OBSERVATION OF "FREE-FIELD" BEHAVIOR AS A METHOD IN THE STUDY AND CLINICAL ASSESSMENT OF MBD CHILDREN

In standard psychologic examinations, children are given particular tasks, which generally require specific reactions to specific stimuli. Reliability of results depends on the child's ability and willingness to maintain a constant level and direction of attention and task orientation during the assessment period. Otherwise, the results do not constitute a valid estimation of the child's abilities.

MBD children often show behavioral disturbances such as hyperactivity, distractibility, and impulsiveness, which are particularly disturbing to the performance of assigned tasks.[10] Yet these are exactly the aspects of maladaptive behavior that the parents and teachers often complain about. They should be closely observed and systematically analyzed instead of being dismissed as "irritating" epiphenomena.

The method of observation and analysis of behavior of the "freely moving" child in a standardized environment is particularly applicable to the study and clinical assessment of children with behavioral disorders. With the proposed approach, such behaviors can be studied in the context of the child's total behavioral repertoire, and their interactions as well as their role in the child's relation to his environment can be evaluated.

Clinical Application of the Method of "Free-field" Observation

In a report in 1955 entitled "The Hyperkinetic Syndrome in Epileptic Children," Ounsted described his first attempts to "crudely quantitate the defects of attention" by "letting the child run wild in the consulting room and recording and timing the duration of different activities carried out by the unfettered child."[10]

To quote Ounsted:

> The child was released in a clinic side-room containing a small number of objects—wooden spatulae, an old tin, a teddy, some paper, a couch with blankets, etc. The mother, nurse, and doctor stood silent and made no interventions. Each activity made by the child was noted, and the duration of each line of behavior was timed. Observations continued for five to fifteen minutes at each visit. The conditions of test were occasionally varied by making the test in more complex environments.[18]

Hutt, Hutt, and Ounsted developed the method further by designing an observation room with a one-way screen, and a block pattern on the floor, so that systematic observation and registration of movement patterns could be obtained. Using this technique, they studied the free-field behavior in groups of children "with and without upper central nervous system lesions."[11] They observed brain-damaged children and controls (see the original report for the exact description of the groups) individually in four situations of increasing complexity: with the room empty, with only blocks present, with blocks and a passive observer, with blocks and an actively participating observer. Behaviors such as locomotion, attention span, and manipulation of fixtures were quantitatively scored from audio-tape recordings and film. Some interesting differences between brain-damaged children and controls emerged: (1) Controls showed visual exploration/inspection before they entered into a new activity, whereas BD's started to manipulate the objects without prior visual inspection. (2) So-called "irrelevant movements" were found in BD's in each of the four situations; in controls, only in the situation "alone in the empty room." (3) Brain-damaged children's behavior remained approximately the same, irrespective of the specific characteristics of the environment, whereas in controls, behavior was adapted to the particular structure of the environment. (4) BD's and controls were discriminated most clearly in the more complex situations. In relatively simple situations (e.g., alone in empty room), no differences were found between these groups.

The groups were small and composed of children with a wide variety of disorders (both were hospital groups; no base rates from normal children were reported). Therefore, generalizations from these findings are difficult. However, the results suggested that looking for these sorts of relationships might be relevant in the assessment of, and research into, minor brain dysfunction.

"Free-field" Observations in Relation to the MBD Problem

Interest in interrelationships between minor neurologic dysfunction and behavior led to the application of free-field observation as part of a follow-up project in the Department of Developmental Neurology in Groningen.[14,15] Approximately 160 pre-

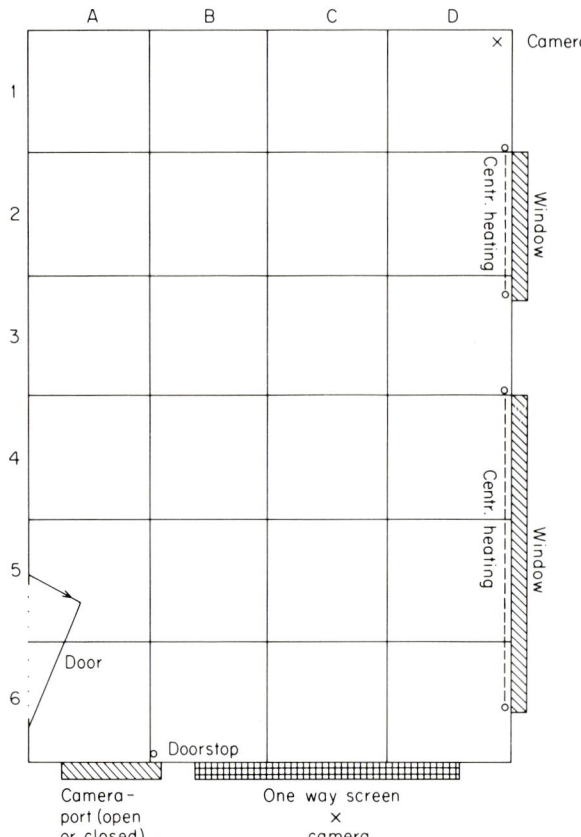

Fig. 2. Plan of the observation room in the Department of Developmental Neurology, University Hospital, Groningen. The squares represent the block pattern on the floor. Each square is 80 × 80 cm.

school children were observed individually in a standard playroom with a block pattern on the floor (Fig. 2).

Each child was observed in six experimental conditions, always in the following sequence: (1) Together with the mother in the empty room (3 min); (2) alone in the empty room (3 min); (3) with a box of blocks and a passive observer (10 min); (4) alone in the empty room (3 min); (5) alone with a variety of toys (15 min); and (6) alone with only one "nonmotivating" toy (5 min).

In all experimental conditions the child was allowed to move around freely. Videotape recordings were made from behind a one-way mirror, as well as from a fixed camera in the room; sound was recorded by a hidden microphone.

Aspects of motor, visual, and verbal behavior, such as those listed in Table 2, were scored from video–audio tapes. While the toys were present, additional scores were given for level of play activity and number of play objects handled by the child. Contact with the mother was scored by categories listed at the bottom of Table 2. This approach permitted a detailed description and analysis of the behavioral repertoire and provided a good opportunity for estimating the reliability of the scoring procedures.

Based on our experience with this technique, we will discuss some methodologic problems and possible applications of free-field observations, with particular reference to the topic of MBD. First, we will point out how systematic variations in the environ-

Table 2. Categories Applied in the Observation of "Free-field" Behavior*

Behavioral Category	Operationalization	Example
Locomotion	Number of "blocks" covered	
Postures	Number of times a posture is observed from a list of postural categories	Standing upright, lying
Types of movement	Number of times a type of movement is observed from a predetermined list	Walking, hopping
Object manipulations	Number of times the child manipulates fixtures in the room (stool included)	Tapping the radiator, twisting the doorstop
Self-manipulations	Number of times the child manipulates his own body or clothes	Scratching his face, fumbling in pocket
Gestures	Number of times nonverbal communicative movements are observed	Pointing at an object, arm movements in relation to verbalization
Additional movements	Number of times movements that are not part of movement patterns of locomotion manipulation or communication are observed[†]	Waving his arms, rocking
Visual fixations	Number of times the child looks at an object for 1 sec or longer	
Visual scanning	Number of times the child looks around without focusing a specific object for 1 sec or longer	
Spatial contact with mother	Number of 10-sec epochs in which the child covers a block adjacent to block a-4 (see Fig. 2)	
Visual contact with mother	Number of 10-sec epochs in which the child looks at the mother for 1 sec or longer	
Tactile contact with mother	Number of 10-sec epochs in which the child touches the mother	
Verbal contact with mother	Number of 10-sec epochs in which the child talks to the mother	

*This categorization is partly based on the work of Berkson[3] and Hutt et al.[11]
[†]Movements toward the one-way mirror are scored in a separate category.

ment may be useful for assessing the adaptive behavior of MBD children. Second, we will outline some of the limiting factors that must be considered in designing observational studies and some of the behavioral categories that must be included in studies of minimal brain dysfunction. Finally, consideration will be given to the problem of focusing on specific units of behavior abstracted from the context of the behavioral repertoire.

The Structure of the Environment

Since behavior is strongly influenced by the structure of the immediate environment, important information about the child's adaptive behavior can be obtained by systematically varying the social or physical characteristics of the child's surroundings. In this way it can be determined how particular features of the situation influence the child's selection of stimulus objects.

The following factors seem to be particularly relevant for the study of children with minimal brain dysfunction.

Novelty vs. Familiarity: The novelty of the environment as an experimental variable contributes considerably to the variance in exploratory activity and contact behavior. This has been demonstrated in different studies, e.g., by Rheingold involving 11-mo-old infants,[24] and by Kalverboer involving 5-yr-old children.[13]

Answers to the following types of questions can contribute to our understanding of adaptive disorders in MBD children.

(1) Does the child start with the visual scanning of the environment or with the fixation on particular features before he starts moving around and manipulating objects?

(2) Is there a gradual change with time in the kinds of exploration and contact behavior? Does the child, for example, stay close to the "security figure" at first, and gradually become more involved in exploratory activity?

(3) Is the child quickly "satiated" by the environment (as indicated by a decline in visual and manipulatory exploration) or is he involved in exploring the room over an extended period?

(4) Does the child's behavior suggest emotional stress in the initial or later phases of the observation?

(5) What are the characteristics of the interaction between a social figure and the child in a relatively unfamiliar situation?

The objectivity with which these questions can be answered will depend on the choice of categories and on the extent to which they are defined in operational terms. (See section entitled "The Choice of Behavioral Categories.") In Table 2, variables are presented as they were applied in our studies. They allow for a relatively refined measurement of contact behavior (spatial, tactile, visual, verbal) and exploratory activity (visual, manipulative, locomotory).

Presence or Absence of Social Figure(s): Whether or not social figures participate in the child's activities, and the nature of the relationship to the child (e.g., parent, stranger, another child), appear to be important variables.

Hutt et al. found that the presence of an observer had an effect on exploratory and play behavior in the control group but not in a group of MBD children.[11] In our studies of a group of normal preschool children, we found that the presence of the mother had a strong effect on the temporal pattern of exploratory behavior in a novel environment: In the presence of the mother the child engaged in intensive exploration of the unfurnished, unfamiliar room, which lasted about 1 min and then stopped abruptly. When the mother was absent the same child continued in his exploratory behavior for the entire 3-min observation period.[13]

In another study on relationships between neurologic variables and free-field behavior, girls with more minor neurologic signs tended to explore the room more freely than girls with fewer signs: The latter group tended to stay closer to the mother and to show more manipulation of their own body and clothes. In boys, no such differences were found.[14,15]

These examples illustrate the relevance of the social figure as a variable in the study of children with MBD. Many of the difficulties reported by parents arise in the social context. Although one must be careful in generalizing from laboratory settings to everyday situations, standardized observations may nevertheless provide useful additional information about the mechanisms at work in the social interaction of children with MBD.

The Presence and Type of Additional Material(s): Observation in play situations can give important information on the child's selective capacities and level of functioning.

In situations with many different toys, certain aspects of selective behavior can be closely studied in detail—for example, the number of toys handled by the child per time unit, the relationship between motor activity and play behavior (e.g., is the locomotion part of the play behavior or does it interfere with play?), sudden changes in type and level of play activity, etc.

Differences in the child's behavior determined by the homogeneity or heterogeneity of play material may indicate how well the child can cope with distracting elements in the immediate environment.

In our studies, the attractiveness of the play objects proved to be a powerful variable for discriminating between boys with and without neurologic signs. The boys with neurologic signs played for a longer time and more intensely in a situation with one nonmotivating toy than boys without neurologic signs.[14,15] The capacity to tolerate mild degrees of "sensory deprivation" is an important aspect of adaptation to school situations as we know them. Observations of the kind described may give relevant information on the child's capacity to cope with such deprivation.

Limiting Factors in Designing Observational Studies

In the previous paragraphs, factors are mentioned that can be varied systematically in order to study behavior in variously structured situations. A large number of other factors may affect a child's behavior and must also be standardized or controlled as much as possible. These include the following:

(1) Minor variations in *experimental instructions*, which may dramatically affect the behavior of the child, because they influence his expectation. For example, does he expect to stay with the mother or to be separated from her, to play with attractive toys or to be examined by a doctor, to go home after a short or a long time? In a similar way, parents can influence the child's expectations and, thus, his behavior in the experimental situation.

(2) Particular *"fixed" characteristics of the laboratory setting* may also influence the child's behavior: Is the room soundproof? Is there a one-way screen or a block pattern on the floor? What sort of fixtures are present? Such factors must be taken into ac-

count in the design of a study, since they may have differential effects on the groups being compared. For example, in our preschool groups we observed that the presence of a one-way screen had quite a different effect on the behavior of boys and girls.[13] In a situation with the mother in the unfamiliar room, boys showed more movement toward the one-way screen and more manipulation of it than girls. Such differential effects must be recognized in the interpretation of the data. Even in well-controlled laboratory studies, it is sometimes overlooked that particular features of the environment may affect children quite differently.

(3) Also of particular importance is the order in which the different observational conditions are arranged. We observed that the child's introduction to the observation room strongly affected his behavior in the course of the observation. When there was the opportunity for the child to become acquainted with the environment in the presence of the mother, the child was less easily upset during the rest of the observation, than when the child had been put alone in the unfamiliar room. Furthermore, we found that many preschool children felt very upset when left alone in a novel environment.

In the study of young children, it is especially important to proceed gradually from conditions in which the child feels secure through the presence of or the access to a supporting figure, to conditions in which such a figure is absent. As a consequence it is often impossible to randomize the order of observations systematically.

From the foregoing it should be clear that standardization of design, procedure, and assessment of results is imperative. Moreover, one has to be most careful in making generalizations from results obtained in specific circumstances to behavior in other situations.

The Choice of Behavioral Categories

The behavioral categories to be applied will depend on the types of problems being considered. Conversely, the classification system will limit the kinds of questions that can be answered. The choice of a classification system will vary according to one's interest in the "morphology," the function, or the causation of behavioral patterns (a sophisticated discussion of classification problems is given in Hinde[8,9]). Two examples will be used for illustration.

(1) Quantitative assessment of locomotion, such as counting the number of squares traversed by the child, provides information about one particular aspect of motor activity. However, it tells us nothing about the function of motor behavior in relation to the environment. Such an assessment will not reveal whether the locomotion was part of the pattern of "specific exploration" (defined by Berlyne[4] as "behavior directed at different features of the environment to afford access to environmental information, not previously available") or part of the pattern of "diversive exploration" (defined by Berlyne as "behavior in which the environment or the own body is used to vary sensory input"). The function of the locomotion can only be determined if other variables—manipulation of fixtures, visual scanning or fixation of features of the environment, etc.—are recorded simultaneously.

(2) In our observational studies of preschool children, we found that girls followed a different strategy in obtaining information about their environment than boys. In girls, visual exploration tended to change over time from scanning to the fixation of particular features, whereas in boys the order was reversed. This finding could only be

obtained because "visual scanning" and "visual fixation" were scored as distinct categories rather than as a general category of "visual exploration."

A detailed classification of the behavioral repertoire permits one to determine the functional significance of particular behaviors. This is especially relevant for complex phenomena such as hyperactivity and disorders in selective attention, where a simultaneous assessment of several aspects of the behavior pattern in relation to environmental features is essential. The use of audio-visual recordings increases the power of the method considerably because it makes possible a reliable analysis of the relation between simultaneously occurring behaviors. Relevant samples of the behavior, which are stored on tape, can also be compared with behavioral samples obtained in other conditions. Slow-motion review of the tapes gives the opportunity for more detailed analyses.

In our studies on the relation between minor neurologic dysfunctions and behavior in preschool children, we classify behavior according to the items listed in Table 2, and observe the children in two types of situations: (1) alone in an empty room, and (2) with the mother in the empty room. With the addition of play materials, we added categories—the number of toys handled by the child, the level of play activity, etc. Our experience is that the behavior disorders commonly associated with minimal brain damage can be quantitatively assessed by using these categories.

For instance, *inconsistency* in motor activity and task-oriented behavior is mentioned as a disorder typical of many MBD children. In the quantitative analysis of free-field behavior, this phenomenon can be reduced to operational terms by scoring the following aspects: predictability of locomotion (regression analysis), changes in body posture and movement pattern (in the empty room or during play activity), changes in level and type of play activity, predictability of contact behavior, etc.

Another handicap in adaptation to the environment that is frequently associated with MBD is *lack of selectivity* in attentional, perceptual, and motor functioning. These aspects can be measured by the application of categories like the following: glancing away from play material, number of objects handled per time unit, latency between looking at objects and handling them, and switching from visual fixation to scanning.

The significance of scores for particular behavioral variables can only be determined by a comparison with baseline values obtained on normal children drawn from adequate reference groups. Furthermore, the relevance of laboratory findings for children's adaptation in actual social and learning situations can only be clarified by validation studies in which objective and relevant criteria are applied. An exception may be when a child is compared with himself (e.g., to evaluate the effects of drugs or psychotherapy). Even here, however, one must exercise care. For the study of any particular child, at least baseline data on the consistency of the behaviors used as dependent variables must be obtained before the evaluation procedure in order to avoid an overinterpretation of the observed differences.

The Problem of "Crucial" Variables

To what extent is it possible and advisable to select specific behavioral variables or specific experimental conditions in the assessment of children with behavioral and learning disorders?

This question is one instance of a general problem, for which there are no simple solutions. The proper answer will depend on the aim of the study or assessment: If the only aim is to discriminate between an experimental and a control group (let us say, between children under a certain drug regime and a group of untreated children), it may be sufficient to know that the specific variable is logically or empirically related to success in treatment. Such a group comparison, however, will not provide new insight into the relationship between treatment and outcome. All that can be concluded is *whether* a certain treatment influences behavior—not *how* it works.

In our studies to date, a few behavioral variables, and some experimental conditions, were particularly sensitive in discriminating between preschool children with and without minor neurologic signs. These were different for boys and girls. In preschool *boys*, the best discriminating variables pertained to consistency of motor or play activity. The experimental condition in which neurologic groups differed most clearly was a situation, lasting 5 min, in which only a nonmotivating toy was present.[14,15] As a group, boys with more neurologic signs were more inconsistent in their behavior and played at a lower level than boys with fewer signs. In preschool *girls*, differences were smaller and less consistent than in boys. The strongest differences were found on variables pertaining to contact behavior and exploratory behavior in the unfamiliar room when the mother was present, girls with fewer signs showing more clinging to the mother and fewer reactions toward aspects of the environment than girls with more signs.

Although these findings may suggest that certain variables are particularly suited to the assessment of MBD children, the observed differences were *between groups* (as is generally true for data given in research reports); the distribution of scores showed large overlaps; and the variables were applied in *specific* experimental conditions. Results from such studies cannot, therefore, be generalized to other situations by any simplistic translation.

Because our knowledge of the complex behavioral and learning problems presented by MBD children is very limited, it is advisable to assess a child's functional repertoire in a number of distinct situations before separating any specific variables from their behavioral context.

Conclusion

The observation and quantitative analysis of free-field behavior is a valuable method in research studies and clinical assessment of behavioral disorders, such as those seen in children with the clinical MBD syndrome. One can focus on aspects of behavior such as motor inconsistency, fluctuations in level of activity and distractibility, which, especially in younger children, may affect the results of psychometric tests and yield unreliable findings. Motor, visual and verbal behaviors can be assessed as part of the total behavioral repertoire, so that insight can be obtained into the complicated interrelationships between behavioral variables. Observation in differently structured situations may provide important information on the child's adaptive capacities.

SUMMARY

Methods have been discussed for the assessment of the degree of nervous integrity in children and for the direct observation and analysis of free-field behavior. Both methods can help in providing insight about the problems of children with learning and behavioral disorders.

The neurologic assessment can demonstrate the degree to which neurologic dysfunctions limit the capacity of the child to cope with the demands of his home and school environments.

The analysis of free-field behavior can give objective and detailed information on aspects of behavior that are directly relevant for the interaction of the child with his social and physical environment.

Both sorts of assessment can assist in planning the proper guidance for the child.

ACKNOWLEDGMENT

Our thanks are due to Dr. J. O'Brien and Professor H. F. R. Prechtl for their invaluable help in the preparation of this manuscript, and to Miss T. Veenstra for her technical assistance.

REFERENCES

1. Abercrombie, M. L. J., London, R. L., and Tyson, M. C.: Associated movements in normal and physically handicapped children. Dev. Med. Child Neurol. 6:573, 1964.

2. Berges, J., and Lezine, I.: The imitation of gestures. Clinics in Developmental Medicine 18. London, Spastics International Medical Publications/Heinemann Medical, 1965.

3. Berkson, G.: Stereotyped movements of mental defectives, Part 5 (Ward behavior and its relation to an experimental task). Am. J. Ment. Defic. 69:253, 1969.

4. Berlyne, D. E.: Conflict, Arousal and Curiosity. New York, McGraw-Hill, 1960.

5. Connolly, K., and Stratton, P.: Developmental changes in associated movements. Dev. Med. Child Neurol. 10:49, 1968.

6. Eisenberg, L.: Classification and categorization in child psychiatry. Int. J. Psychiatry 3:179, 1967.

7. Fog, E., and Fog, M.: Cerebral inhibition examined by associated movements. In Bax, M., and MacKeith, R. (Eds.): Minimal Cerebral Dysfunction. Clinics in Developmental Medicine 10. London, Spastics International Medical Publications/Heinemann Medical, 1963.

8. Hinde, R. A.: Animal behaviour: A synthesis of ethology and comparative psychology. New York, McGraw-Hill, 1966.

9. —: Problems in the study of the development of social behavior. In Tobach, E., Aronson, L. R., and Shaw, E. (Eds.): The Biology of Development. New York, Academic Press, 1971.

10. Hutt, C., Hutt, S. J., and Ounsted, C.: A method for the study of children's behaviour. Dev. Med. Child Neurol. 5:233, 1963.

11. —, —, and —: The behaviour of children with and without upper C.N.S. lesions. Behaviour 24:246, 1965.

12. Illingworth, R. S.: The Development of the Infant and Young Child; Normal and Abnormal. London, E. & A. Livingstone, 1966.

13. Kalverboer, A. F.: Observation of exploratory behaviour of preschool children alone and in the presence of the mother. Psychiatr. Neurol. Neurochir. 74:43, 1971.

14. —: Observations of free-field behaviour in preschool boys and girls in relation to neurological findings. In Stoelinga, van der Werff ten Bosch (Ed.): Normal and Abnormal Development of Brain and Behaviour. Leiden, Leiden University Press, 1971, p. 187.

15. —, Touwen, B. C. L., and Prechtl, H. F. R.: Infants at risk of minor brain dysfunction. Proceedings MBD Congress. Ann. N. Y. Acad. Sci., in press.

16. McGraw, M. B.: The Neuromuscular Maturation of the Human Infant (reprint ed.). New York, Hafner, 1969.

17. Müller, D.: Neurologische Untersuchung und Diagnostik im Kindesalter. Wien, Springer, 1968.

18. Ounsted, C.: The hyperkinetic syndrome in epileptic children. Lancet 2:303, 1955.

19. Paine, R. S., and Oppé, T. E.: Neurological examination of children. Clinics in Developmental Medicine 21/22. London, Spastics International Medical Publications/Heinemann Medical, 1966.

20. Prechtl, H. F. R.: Problems of behavioral studies in the newborn infant. In Lehrman, D. S., Hinde, R. A., and Shaw, E. (Eds.): Advances in the Study of Behavior, Vol. I. New York, Academic Press, 1965, p. 75.

21. —: Hazards of over-simplification. Dev. Med. Child Neurol. 12:522, 1970.

22. —: Strategy and validity of early detection of neurological dysfunction. Symposium series of Institute for Research into Mental Retardation. Oxford, Pergamon Press, 1972, p. 41.

23. —, and Beintema, D. J.: The neurological examination of the fullterm newborn infant. Clinics in Developmental Medicine 12. London, Spastics International Medical Publications/ Heinemann Medical, 1964.

24. Rheingold, H. L.: The effect of a strange

environment on the behaviour of infants. *In* Foss, B. M. (Ed.): Determinants of Infant Behaviour, Vol. 4. London, Methuen, 1969.

25. Rutter, M., Graham, P., and Yule, W.: A neuropsychiatric study in childhood. Clinics in Developmental Medicine 35/36. London, Spastics International Medical Publications/Heinemann Medical, 1970.

26. Touwen, B. C. L.: A study of the development of some motor phenomena in infancy. Dev. Med. Child Neurol. 13:435, 1971.

27. —: Neurological long-term prognosis of pre- and perinatal complications. XIII International Congress of Pediatrics, Vienna, 1971, in press.

28. —, and Prechtl, H. F. R.: The neurological examination of the child with minor nervous dysfunction. Clinics in Developmental Medicine 38. London, Spastics International Medical Publications/Heinemann Medical, 1970.

29. Zazzo, R. (Ed.): Manual pour l'Examination Psychologique de l'Enfant. Neuchâtel, De la Cheux et Niestlé, 1960.

The Hyperkinetic Syndrome

John E. O'Malley, M.D., and Leon Eisenberg, M.D.

THE HYPERKINETIC SYNDROME refers to a symptom constellation of motor restlessness, impulsivity, short attention span, learning difficulties and emotional lability. It may occur alone, but often is seen in conjunction with other psychiatric or neurologic entities in children. Many other terms have been coined in the literature,[14] and some clinicians prefer "minimal brain dysfunction"[3] or "minimal brain damage" because of the association of this behavior complex with "soft" neurologic signs, "organic indicators" on psychologic testing, and a history suggesting biologic rather than psychosocial etiology. However, the World Health Organization prefers "hyperkinetic syndrome" because the term does not imply etiology.[20] The American Psychiatric Association lists this behavior profile under the category of "hyperkinetic reaction of childhood."[6] Whatever the terminology, the clinician must rely solely on his diagnostic acumen, since there are no pathognomonic findings.[9]

CLINICAL DESCRIPTION

Typically, the parents seek help for their child because of problem behavior at school. The child, usually a boy and often the firstborn, is in both academic and disciplinary trouble. His mother reports that he can't sit still, will not complete tasks, is disobedient and moody. He has few friends, cannot play well or for prolonged periods of time, and is in more than his share of trouble in the neighborhood.

The pregnancy and birth more often than not were without apparent difficulties. As an infant, he was active and irritable. As soon as he was able to climb out of the crib and walk, the mother felt that she was following an unleashed tornado. He always ran, needed a watchful eye to protect him and the objects around him from disaster, and never seemed to tire. He was slow in learning to button his clothes and tie his shoes, he may have had minor speech problems, and his handwriting is still illegible. It is difficult to get him to bed, and difficult to get him up. He is often moody in the morning, slow to get started, unable to get dressed and off to school without increasingly firm reminders. Throughout his school years there have been reports about his poor behavior. He disturbed the class, did not respond to directions, and needed constant supervision. The school continues to observe that he is restless, irritable, distractible, inattentive, easily frustrated, and far behind in his work. He does better when isolated from peers, in one-to-one encounters, and on shorter school days. Special education may have been recommended for him.

The family history often suggests a similar behavior pattern in the child's father or sibling. The physical examination reveals little more than clumsiness, equivocal choreiform movements, and some difficulty in performing skilled motor acts. Conversation with the child elicits only complaints about unfair teachers and laments that nobody likes him. A psychiatric interview may suggest a poor self-image, low self-esteem and denial of troubles at school (or at least his involvement in the trouble). Characteristi-

---

Reprint requests should be addressed to John E. O'Malley, M.D., Major, M.C. United States Army, Chief of Outpatient Psychiatry, Madigan General Hospital, Tacoma, Wash. 98431.

cally, he may not be restless in the office with a sympathetic adult and a minimum of other stimuli (although the waiting room may be in a shambles). His behavior falls apart when he is faced with a group situation, or academic pressures, or when alternatives are presented. The physician may surmise that the child would do fine in a dimly lit, soundproof, empty room.

Laboratory findings are virtually nonexistent. Electroencephalographic recordings are normal or may reveal "more slow waves than normal for age." Psychologic testing reveals normal intelligence (sometimes with a discrepancy between verbal and performance tasks), confirms the academic lag, and sometimes exposes perceptual (visual-motor) abnormalities.

With the paucity of objective criteria and the lack of pathognomonic findings, the clinician must make the diagnosis on the basis of history and the symptom complex as reported by parents and teachers. There are no special tests or examinations that will yield the diagnosis. However, they *can* help in the careful educational planning that may be needed.

PREVALENCE

The reported prevalence of the hyperkinetic syndrome will vary greatly with the restrictiveness or broadness of the criteria employed. Since it is a condition that defies precise definition, lacks pathognomonic findings, and is a matter of some controversy, prevalence is difficult to establish. Before comparisons can be made, the studies that have been done must be viewed by criteria of definitions and by age distribution.

According to WHO criteria for diagnosis, the term "hyperkinetic syndrome" should be applied only if other significant psychopathology is absent. Thus, the prevalence of the syndrome as a diagnosis will be much lower than as a symptom complex because of its frequent association with other neuropsychiatric disorders, which may take precedence for administrative reasons. What can be said is that complaints about this symptom cluster from parents and teachers are common, and especially frequent among children referred to psychiatric clinics.

Prechtl and Stemmer[17] reported from the Netherlands a prevalence of 20% in boys of elementary-school age, and 10% in girls. They defined a "choreiform syndrome" by the presence of minimal choreiform movements with associated "behavior problems." In addition, 90% of these children had reading difficulties. By using teacher reports of overactivity and short attention span, Stewart[25] found hyperkinesis in 4% of a population of St. Louis grade-school children between the ages of 5 and 11. Huessy[11] conducted a survey of second-grade children in Vermont by using a school questionnaire and found 10% of them to be "hyperkinetic." He also found that of the children considered by teachers to have serious problems, 80% fell into this category. Wender[28] quotes the results of the Montgomery County, Maryland, prevalence study of psychologic disturbance: In a stratified sample of 20% of the population of elementary-school children (approximately 24,000 out of a total of 120,000 children), teacher ratings indicated that restlessness was a "problem" in approximately 15% of the children and decreased attention span in 22%. As Wender aptly points out, "problem" is a rather nonspecific term, but it does suggest that, by teachers' criteria, 5%–20% of school-age children suffer from the "problem of restlessness."

As to the prevalence of the hyperkinetic syndrome in children referred to psychiatric clinics, Wender reported his own experience in which 50% of school-aged children in a university clinic and 50%-65% in a county clinic fell into the category of "minimal brain dysfunction."[28]

Prevalence among boys compared to girls varies from three or four to one[16] to nine to one.[30]

On the other hand, in a study of the total population of 10- and 11-yr-old children living on the Isle of Wight and attending local authority schools—a total of 2199 children—only 2 (1 boy and 1 girl) were classified as having the hyperkinetic syndrome, "although a much larger number showed restlessness or overactivity as part of a conduct or neurotic disorder."[21] The authors surmised that many more would have been identified in a survey of a younger school-aged group and that some of the antisocial cases might have represented outcomes of an earlier hyperkinetic syndrome. In the same report, the authors noted that teachers described 13% of the general school population as "restless" and 32% as showing "poor concentration" whereas the percentages for children with "brain dysfunction" were 32% and 58% respectively. Similar excesses over matched controls were reported for neuroepileptic and psychiatric cases.

NATURAL HISTORY

To be certain that the syndrome reflects a pathologic process rather than a variation of "normal exuberance of childhood," several investigators compared hyperkinetic children to controls in order to test the "realness" of the syndrome. Douglas[7] employed direct classroom observation and found these children to be less attentive and more disruptive than their peers. Campbell[2] compared hyperkinetic children to controls on four "dimensions" of cognitive style and found them to be more impulsive, more field dependent, more distractible, and slower in automatization.

The data on the syndrome are persuasive, but information on outcome has been anecdotal, implied, and filled with mythology. It has been said that these children "outgrow" the syndrome sometime in puberty and, even if untreated, "catch up" with their peers.[8] "Developmental lag" is part of the terminology and a conceptual trap for clinicians. As experience has accumulated, however, it appears less likely that the child simply "outgrows" this syndrome. In a severely ill population, Bond[1] reported bleak results for 85 children following recovery from von Economo's encephalitis. Their behavior was characterized by restlessness, disobedience, aggressiveness, difficulty at home and school. They were followed for a period ranging from 1-9 yr (although this is not clearly stated in the study) and only 20 of the 85 returned to normal functioning. All improved to some degree but 33 "were later taken to state hospitals, schools for feeble minded, or reformatory institutions."

In psychiatric samples, the populations have been too heterogeneous for measuring the outcome of hyperkinetic children.[15,18] Menkes[12] reported on 14 children seen 25 yr earlier in an outpatient psychiatric clinic. These children evidenced hyperactivity, learning disorders and one or more "neurologic signs"—clumsiness, visual-motor impairments, speech difficulty. The term "hyperactivity" included distractibility, short attention span, emotional lability, impulsivity. All had IQs above 70. At follow-up four were hospitalized psychotics, two were retarded and four had been institutionalized at some point in time. Three of the patients, then about 30 yr old, still complained of restlessness; others indicated that restlessness had ceased at age 12-14, although in some it remained until age 21. Hammar[10] in a retrospective study noted that half of the adolescents admitted to the clinic with a history of underachievement had signs of "minimal brain dysfunction." They ranged in age from 12-18 and were characterized as having poor memory retention, short attention span, distractibility, and impulsive behavior; hyperactivity was no longer a problem. In interpreting these data, Wender noted that the sample might have contained many hyperkinetic children now "grown up" and that the findings suggested that although the "hyperkinesis" disappeared, a residual of behavioral problems and underachievement remained.

This impression is supported by the one anterospective study of the most common variant of the hyperkinetic syndrome—a hyperactive child of normal intelligence, referred for learning difficulties or behavior problems and showing no neurologic signs. Weiss et al.[27] reported a 5-yr follow-up study of 64 hyperactive children who met the following criteria: (1) long-term and sustained hyperactivity; (2) 6-13 yr of age; (3) an IQ greater than 84, as measured by the Wechsler Intelligence Scale for Children; (4) not psychotic; (5) no major brain damage or dysfunction such as epilepsy or cerebral palsy, and (6) living at home with at least one parent. Sixty were boys with a mean age of 8.7 at referral and 13.3 at the time of follow-up. Whereas hyperactivity had been the chief complaint on referral, it was no longer so 5 yr later. However, 30% of the 64 mothers reported that restlessness was still present, though not severe. Rating scales and classroom observation of hyperactivity suggested that these children did "not necessarily or entirely outgrow their restlessness, but rather expressed it in less gross or disturbing ways." Distractibility, aggressivity, and emotional immaturity (reported by 70% of mothers) remained prominent. *Eighty per cent of these children had poor academic functioning.* Only 20% of the children had not repeated at least one grade as compared to 85% of the control group. Ten per cent had been in special classrooms, 5% expelled, and only 5% were doing above average work.

Weiss et al. concluded that hyperactivity diminished but that other major handicaps remained, namely, disorders of attention and concentration. Associated with this was chronic underachievement in school despite normal intelligence. These children also demonstrated a significant propensity toward psychopathology with emotional immaturity, inability to attain goals, poor self-image and feelings of hopelessness. They were differentiated from their peers by greater restlessness, aggressivity, and more antisocial acts at time of followup.

Although more anterospective studies are needed for definitive statements of prognosis, it is clear that we cannot say, "All will be well, just bear with it now." We are faced, then, with a syndrome that affects many school-aged children and that has potentially profound implications for their development and success as adults.

ETIOLOGY

Except for the rare child who manifests the syndrome as a result of a noxious agent (lead poisoning, encephalitis, etc.) or brain trauma, the cause has been elusive. Certainly a single cause is unlikely; the behavior is a final common pathway for the expression of diverse pathologies. We still lack the sophistication to differentiate subgroups, to tease out differences, and to refine the measurements necessary for etiologic inference. Clinical experience suggests that the syndrome runs in families, and a foster care study[22] implies a genetic basis. Complications of pregnancy and parturition, although generally unreliable clinically when reported by mothers,[31] have been shown to be associated with overactive, disorganized behavior in an epidemiologic study of a school guidance referral group;[19] yet a matched comparison of the pediatric histories of hyperkinetic versus other clinic patients failed to reveal reliable differences.[13] Wender[28] has proposed that there is an underlying defect in the function of monoaminergic neurons; the therapeutic effectiveness of sympathomimetic drugs was ascribed to their known ability to amplify noradrenergic effects in the central nervous system. Testing this hypothesis is difficult because we lack the methods for measuring central neurotransmitters in human subjects. Peripheral metabolism and physiology may not reflect central effects.[29] Warren et al.[26] have reported that there was no evidence of aneuploidy or other chromosome abnormality in 96 patients examined. Satterfield[23] found that hyperkinetic children had lower basal skin conductance, fewer and smaller nonspecific GSRs, and smaller specific GSRs than those of normal children. He proposed that hyperkinetic behavior might be due to a lowered excitability of the mid-brain reticular activating system. The increased activity, then, is viewed as an attempt to increase proprioceptive and exteroceptive sensory input.

Although these hypotheses are provocative, the pathogenesis remains unknown. Explanations are heuristic and continued research is needed.

HYPERKINESIS

The relationship between hyperkinesis and cognitive function needs clarification. Early in the developmental sequence, motor activity initially characterizes a child's behavior. From rolling over to walking to the most skilled, fine movements, a sequence is established and norms attained. We are concerned about a child who does not walk by the age of two, or who is listless and flaccid as an infant. Speech development follows an orderly course from simple words to complex syntactical structure. However, for cognitive functions to occur, such as learning complex skills (reading), the child must be able to limit his motor activity, discern relevant stimuli, ignore irrelevant stimuli, and focus his attention. The more he is unable to sit still, attend to a task, and focus his senses on relevant stimuli, the less likely it is that he will be able to learn. A child who is distracted by a noise outside the classroom, or the guinea pig on the desk, or one of a hundred other things, cannot attend to a given specific task. It is not "boredom" that distracts him; it is driven, motoric behavior that doesn't allow him to attend. It is as if his accelerator pedal is stuck to the floor, not allowing him to stop for a red light, or for that matter, to realize that the red light is of any more significance than a blade of grass he passes by.

There are studies that suggest that *total* activity does not differ between hyperkinetic children and normal children. What differs is the ability to brake the activity at appropriate times, as in school. Activity in normal children becomes increasingly goal-directed with age; hyperactive children lack such goal-directedness.

Of course, there are moments when hyperactive children are still and when normal children are hyperactive. If there is a minimal amount of distraction, hyperkinetic children typically can watch a television program. Television can be mesmerizing; their attention is totally directed to the flickering screen. On the other hand, normoactive children, when fatigued, recovering from an illness, or involuntarily confined in church, a theater, or involved in other adult activities, may look like hyperkinetic children. It is clear, however, that such activities hold little interest for them and have minimal comprehensibility. Likewise, in extremely stimulating environments like a circus, baseball game, or chaotic home situation, their cognitive abilities become overloaded and the spill-off is seen in motor behavior. What differentiates normal children and hyperkinetic children is the return to normal activity levels, goal-directed behavior, and appropriate attention when the stimulus overload is removed; hyperkinetic children do not return to such a base line. Stimuli have to be almost completely removed before such a base line is reached.

TREATMENT

Treatment presupposes an initial recognition of the problem. This requires the careful evaluation of parent histories, teacher reports, and the social context in which the behavior profile occurs. Once the diagnosis is made, three treatment modalities in various combinations are available. How much, how often, and which ones to choose are the challenges to the clinician and require his consideration long after the diagnosis is made.

Environmental Manipulation

The principles are straightforward: decreasing the amount of extraneous stimuli, decreasing the alternatives, and encouraging patterns of behavior. Avoiding situations known to cause difficulty such as restaurants, theaters, and the like can be helpful. Setting out school clothes the night before, having a separate bedroom from siblings, having breakfast ready, avoiding long trips to school, having play clothes ready upon return from school—all can be suggested within the constraints on the family. Whatever the limitations, the principles can be translated into practical suggestions for parents.

The school setting and its adaptability to the needs of the child are other areas of the environment that will need close attention. It is in planning for schooling that psychologic testing is of the most benefit. The appropriate remedial program—for example, in reading—can be planned wisely and intelligently in cooperation with the school. The child may need a special reading class, an individual tutor at school or at home, or other special services offered by the school. If they are not available, simple classroom changes can help; isolating the child from distractions, establishing a "quiet place" for sanctuary for the child if necessary, and using teacher assistants and aides in an individual relationship can be suggested. These children do better in a structured, closed classroom setting.

Involvement in group activities cannot and should not be stopped. However, providing more structure can help. Boys' clubs, the YMCA, and other organizations can provide adult-supervised, structured activities in which the child can learn to cope with situations that are troublesome.

Medication

By far the most effective treatment modality is the use of the stimulants dextroamphetamine and methylphenidate.[4,5,24] These agents suppress overactivity and impulsivity and lengthen attention span. (This effect is "paradoxical" when compared to adult patients where activity is increased.) Why this should be so for these children simply is not known. Either agent may be used initially since there is little difference between them. Occasionally, a child will respond to one and not the other. Dosage is a very individual matter from child to child, but with either drug, a thorough trial should be undertaken.

The initial dose is 5 mg dextroamphetamine or 10 mg methylphenidate given once in the morning. This can be increased every two or three days to a maximum of 40 mg dextroamphetamine or 80 mg methylphenidate divided into morning and noontime doses. On this regime $\frac{2}{3}$-$\frac{3}{4}$ of hyperkinetic children will show marked-to-moderate improvement.[9] Usually improvement is unequivocal. Missing a single dose will bring the child back to his base line and be immediately noticed by parents and teachers.

The most common side effects are insomnia and anorexia. Both effects may diminish in a week or so even if the dose remains the same. It should be remembered that tolerance is the limiting factor in the use of these agents for weight control. Insomnia is the reason for using only two doses a day, with the second to be given at noon. The drug can be given with meals if anorexia remains a problem. Weight charts can be kept. It is not uncommon for a child to lose a few pounds and then regain the weight appropriate for his age. If weight loss or lack of sleep persists, dosage will have to be lowered; benefits must be titrated with the side effects. Psychotic reactions have been reported[9] but are extremely rare and cease with discontinuation of the drug.

The child may need prolonged treatment with these agents. Although tolerance (requiring dose increments) is sometimes seen, it is unusual. There has been no evidence of habituation to these agents in children; even after several years of use, the child demonstrates no withdrawal if pills are missed from one day to the next. The dilemma is to know when to discontinue the medication after a good result is maintained. It is our practice to stop the medication during long school vacations (including the summer), and not to reinstitute it until after the child has returned to school and demonstrates evidence of return of the syndrome. This means that the physician must be willing to follow the child carefully until he no longer evidences the syndrome. Treatment may be required for as long as 3–5 yr, but in mild cases no more than 6 mo may be necessary.

It is important to note that although these drugs alleviate the motor and attentional disorders that interfere with learning, they do not produce learning; they make it possible to learn. These drugs are not an end in themselves; all of the treatment modalities suggested must be included if the child is to benefit completely. Parent counseling, family therapy, and remedial education will all have to be instituted in one form or another if the child is to resume a normal developmental pathway.

Other drugs have been used with varying success. One of the most promising appears to be imipramine, but carefully controlled studies are lacking. Pemoline, a stimulant still unavailable commercially, has the advantage of once-a-day dosage. There are reports of the use of lithium carbonate[32] and tranquilizers[24,32] with varying degrees of benefit. More experience is needed to evaluate their usefulness. Certainly such agents should be used with the child who does not respond to stimulants.

Psychotherapy

Individual psychotherapy per se is not adequate to treat hyperkinetic children unless the other necessary treatments are employed at the same time. No psychiatrist would think of treating a diabetic without insulin to relieve his diabetes, but he certainly would treat the patient for the conflicts, feelings, and secondary emotional manifestations that might be a result of his diabetes or contribute to its exacerbation. Psychotherapy, indeed, can be useful as an adjunct to other methods. The child may need help with his self-image and self-esteem, and in understanding that he is not at fault.

He will need to acquire skills in dealing with peers. If medication is effective and the appropriate remedial education begun, he may need help accepting his new role and feeling of well-being. Old patterns of behavior will need to be discarded and new, more appropriate ones, formed.

Family therapy and counseling may also be important. The family will need assistance in understanding his behavior, guidance in changing his environment, and aid in viewing the child in a new role. If he has responded to medication, he may no longer be the family scapegoat that he previously had been. "He is a different child" is a frequent comment when response to medicine is dramatic. A "different" child will require a "different" family orientation.

FOLLOW-UP STUDY

The need for follow-up study cannot be overstated. The hyperkinetic syndrome is a chronic disorder requiring long-term, closely monitored care, much like epilepsy. Because medication often provides a dramatic, immediate improvement in behavior, follow-up is all too often neglected. What is frequently forgotten with the short-term diminution of hyperactivity is the long-term learning problems, which need careful consideration. Also ignored are the secondary problems of negative self-image, inappropriate behavior patterns, and readjustment to peers. Long-term follow-up studies of children on stimulants are lacking but are sorely needed for informed clinical practice.

CONCLUSION

The hyperkinetic syndrome, characterized by motor restlessness, short attention span, poor impulse control, learning difficulties, and emotional lability, affects 5%–10% of school-aged children. It is a serious, chronic abnormality that needs careful diagnostic evaluation and appropriate therapeutic intervention over a prolonged period of time. To dismiss the syndrome because the label may be misapplied is to deny these children a chance for healthy development. To suggest that the use of stimulant drugs is an attempt to control minds and make children obedient robots is nonsense. As stated elsewhere: "Restlessness, distractibility and impulsivity are constraints on freedom, not freedom: the child is not free to behave; he is driven. Is a child whose attention is commanded by every passing sight and sound, meaningful and meaningless alike, to be considered 'independent'? Is a child who is not learning to read, when most of his classmates are, in any sense expressing 'creativity'?"[9] Stimulant drugs allow learning to occur, make it possible for a child to concentrate, to reflect on his behavior; they do not make it happen, they allow it to happen. As with any other potent agent, indiscriminate use, misuse, and inadequate follow-up must be avoided. But to abjure drug therapy is to deny an effective mode of treatment for children at serious risk for major psychopathology.

The appropriate use not only of stimulant drugs, but also of environmental manipulation and psychotherapeutic techniques is imperative. Continued, careful follow-up is imperative, with adjustments in medication, the introduction of family counseling, and changes in educational remediation at periodic intervals as necessary. Without continuing medical and educational care, the emerging evidence suggests an unrelenting downhill course. With judicious use of the tools available to us, such children can develop into healthy and productive adults.

REFERENCES

1. Bond, E. D., and Smith, L. H.: Postencephalitic behavior disorders: A ten-year review of Franklin School. Am. J. Psychiatry 92:17, 1935.
2. Campbell, S. B., Douglas, V. I., and Morgenstern, G.: Cognitive styles in hyperactive children and the effect of methylphenidate. J. Child Psychol. Psychiatry 12:55, 1971.
3. Clements, S. D., and Peters, J. E.: Minimal brain dysfunction in the school-age child. Arch. Gen. Psychiatry 6:185, 1962.
4. Conners, C. K., and Eisenberg, L.: The effect of methylphenidate on symptomatology and learning in disturbed children. Am. J. Psychiatry 120:458, 1963.
5. —, Eisenberg, L., and Barcai, A.: Effect of dextroamphetamine in children. Arch. Gen. Psychiatry 17:478, 1967.
6. Diagnostic and Statistical Manual of Mental Disorders (DSM-II), Washington, D.C., American Psychiatric Association, 1968.
7. Douglas, V. I., Weiss, G., and Minde, K.: Learning disabilities in hyperactive children and the effect of methylphenidate. Can. J. Psychol. 10:201, 1969.
8. Eisenberg, L.: The management of the hyperkinetic child. Dev. Med. Child Neurol. 8:593, 1966.
9. —: Behavior modification by drugs. III. The clinical use of stimulant drugs in children. Pediatrics 49:709, 1972.
10. Hammar, S. L.: School underachievement in the adolescent: A review of 73 cases. Pediatrics 40:373, 1967.
11. Huessy, H. R.: Study of the prevalence and therapy of the hyperkinetic syndrome in public school children in rural Vermont. Acta Paedopsychiat. 34:130, 1967.
12. Menkes, M., Rowe, J. S., and Menkes, J. H.: A twenty-five year follow-up study on the hyperkinetic child with minimal brain dysfunction. Pediatrics 39:393, 1967.
13. Minde, K., Webb, G., and Sykes, D.: Studies on the hyperactive child. VI. Prenatal and paranatal factors associated with hyperactivity. Dev. Med. Child Neurol. 10:355, 1968.
14. Minimal Brain Dysfunction in Children. NINDS Monograph No. 3, Part One, 1966.
15. Morris, H. H., Escoll, P. J., and Wexler, R.: Aggressive behavior disorders of childhood: A follow-up study. Am. J. Psychiatry 112:991, 1956.
16. Paine, R. S., Werry, J. S., and Quay, H. C.: A study of minimal brain dysfunction. Dev. Med. Child Neurol. 10:505, 1968.
17. Prechtl, H. F. R., and Stemmer, C. J.: The choreiform syndrome in children. Dev. Med. Child Neurol. 4:119, 1962.
18. Robins, L.: Deviant Children Grown Up. Baltimore, Williams & Wilkins, 1966.
19. Rogers, M. E., Lilienfeld, A. M., and Pasamanick, B.: Prenatal and paranatal factors in the development of childhood behavior disorders. Acta Psychiatr. Neurol. Scand. (Suppl.) 102, 1955.
20. Rutter, M., Lebovici, S., Eisenberg, L., Sneznevskij, A. V., Sadoun, R., Brooke, E., and Lin, T. S.: A hi-axial classification of mental disorders in childhood. J. Child Psychol. Psychiatry 10:41, 1969.
21. —, Tizard, J., and Whitmore, K.: Education, Health and Behavior. London, Longman, 1970.
22. Safer, D. J.: The familial incidence of minimal brain dysfunction. Unpublished manuscript, 1971.
23. Satterfield, J. H., and Dawson, M. E.: Electrodermal correlates of hyperactivity in children. Psychophysiology 8:191, 1971.
24. Sprague, R. L., Barnes, K. R., and Werry, J. S.: Methylphenidate and thioridazine: Learning, reaction time, activity and classroom behavior in disturbed children. Am. J. Orthopsychiatry 40:615, 1970.
25. Stewart, M., Ferris, A., Pitts, N., and Craig, A. G.: The hyperactive child syndrome. Am. J. Orthopsychiatry 36:861, 1966.
26. Warren, R. J., Karduck, W. A., Bussaratid, S., Stewart, M. A., and Sly, W. S.: The hyperactive child syndrome: Normal chromosome findings. Arch. Gen. Psychiatry 24:161, 1971.
27. Weiss, G., Minde, K., Werry, J. S., Douglas, V., and Nemeth, E.: Studies on the hyperactive child. VIII. Five-year follow-up. Arch. Gen. Psychiatry 24:409, 1971.
28. Wender, P. H.: Minimal Brain Dysfunction in Children. New York, Wiley-Interscience, 1971.
29. —, Epstein, R. S., Koplin, I. J., and Gordon, E. K.: Urinary monamine metabolite in children with minimal brain dysfunction. Am. J. Psychiatry 127:1411, 1971.
30. Werry, J. S.: Studies on the hyperactive child: An empirical analysis of the minimal brain dysfunction syndrome. Arch. Gen. Psychiatry 19:9, 1968.
31. —, Weiss, G., and Douglas, V.: Studies on the hyperactive child. I. Some preliminary findings. Can. Psychiatr. Assoc. J. 9:120, 1964.
32. Whitehead, P. L., and Clark, L. D.: Effect of lithium carbonate, placebo, and thioridazine on hyperactive children. Am. J. Psychiatry 127:6, 1970.

Functional Implications of the Minimal Brain Damage Syndrome

Peter H. Wolff, M.D., and Irving Hurwitz, Ph.D.

The definitions and functional implications of minimal brain damage and synonymous diagnostic terms are examined and compared. A study exploring the relation of choreiform movements to behavior disturbances in a classroom of presumably normal children was reported. The results suggest that more extensive systematic studies of the same kind will be necessary before it can be determined whether the confused, but nevertheless extensive, domain of mixed behavioral and neurologic disabilities in school-age children belong to one global syndrome, or should be classified separately according to differences in etiology, functional significance, and response to therapeutic intervention.

> When a ... theory grows old and stiff (as periodically it does, and then has to be rejuvenated), men begin to take its categories and subcategories for granted, and presently forget where in fact these come from, and assume that these have some intrinsic and ultimate cosmic value in themselves. The concepts are often pretty thin by that time, little more than names with a cosmic glow about them. Such has been the fate of many good terms, and some not so good—substance, matter, mind, spirit, God, ego, consciousness, essence, identity, phlogiston, ether, energy, magnetism. As a fallacy this cognitive propensity is sometimes called hypostatization ... when a term or concept begins to demand respect in its own right it is beginning to be hypostatized. The fallacy is often hard to detect, because the process of hypostatization is gradual and rarely complete. The detection is, however, easier once the dogmatic claims of infallibility, self-evidence and indubitability have been recognized as fallacious. All that remains to be done then is *to find the concept's actual significance in terms of multiplicative or structural corroboration....* —Stephen Pepper[21]

THE CONCEPT of minimal brain damage (also called minimal or minor cerebral dysfunction, minimal brain dysfunction, etc.) and its implications for mental development remain as confused today as when the concept was first introduced by Werner and Strauss,[30] and Strauss and Lehtinen.[26] For years, minimal brain damage

---

Work for this presentation was completed while Dr. Wolff was supported by NIMH Career Scientist Award MH-03461, and while Drs. Wolff and Hurwitz were supported by NIMH Research Grant 1 MH-18322.

Reprint requests should be addressed to Peter H. Wolff, M.D., Children's Hospital Medical Center, 300 Longwood Avenue, Boston, Mass. 02115.

was probably the neurologic diagnosis most frequently encountered in pediatric practice.[20] The term gradually lost favor when the qualifier "minimal" was recognized to be devoid of meaning, whereas brain damage was in most cases thought to be undemonstrable by clinical examination[5,13] (see, however, contrary views[14,27] about the clinical neurologic examination as a valid instrument for demonstrating minor neurologic dysfunction). Descriptive terms less burdened with etiologic assumptions, such as "hyperkinesis," "perceptual motor handicaps," "dyslexia," and "learning disability," partially replaced the concept of minimal brain damage syndrome, each formulated to emphasize a particular clinical feature of the overall entity—if indeed such an entity exists. Hyperkinesis referred to the disruptive motor restlessness observed in many of the children;[2,3,9,17,18,31] perceptual motor handicaps accounted for children who had unusual difficulties coordinating fine motor actions and visual perceptions;[6,11,28] learning disability became the term of choice when the fact that many public school children were not receiving an adequate education finally became a matter of general concern.[5,19]

For lack of operational criteria that define the borders of any one entity or differentiate among the various designations, each category gradually extended its domain to encompass children and syndromes in all other categories, until it is now impossible to determine how the diagnosis of minimal brain damage differs from that of hyperkinesis, learning disabilities, or perceptual motor handicaps. Since the terms seem to be applied almost indiscriminately to very similar populations, the question arises whether the confusing and overlapping diagnoses should be replaced by one encompassing concept; or whether some of the descriptive designations should be retained because they refer to functionally and etiologically distinct entities that require further specification in their own right.

As clinical entities, the syndromes of minimal brain damage and hyperkinesis appear to be very similar in scope. Even here, however, the overlap is not complete. Emphasis on motor restlessness as an obligatory criterion will exclude children with minor neurologic signs and behavior disturbances who at the same time show motor *inhibition* (i.e., hypokinesis); thus, they may be deprived of proper medical attention or treatment because they cause no trouble in school or at home.

The diagnosis of minimal brain damage is frequently based on the child's general profile of distractibility, emotional lability, short attention span, clumsiness, and underachievement in school, rather than on any evidence of neurologic deficits.[4,26] Because these diagnostic standards are often vague, the inadmissible diagnostic term "minimal brain damage syndrome without evidence of brain damage" is not uncommon. Since teachers and special educators are by now well informed about the associations between learning disorders and behavior patterns suggestive of nervous dysfunction, a group of children might be diagnosed as having either minimal brain damage or a learning disability, depending on local preference or referral source. Yet, it would be absurd to equate learning disabilities with the minimal brain damage syndrome. Many children with learning disorders demonstrate no evidence of brain damage. While the incidence of neurologic signs is higher in children with learning disabilities than in the general population, the association does not justify the assumption that all learning disorders are caused by manifest or latent brain damage or brain dysfunction. Many children with minor neurologic signs perform in the superior range of academic achievement, and we cannot exclude the possibility that neurologic dysfunction can exist coincidentally in a child with learning difficulties.

If the confusion about the diagnosis were simply "a matter of semantics," any one term would serve as well as any other, provided the terms were first stripped of their excessive meanings. The diagnosis does, however, have major consequences for the choice of treatment as well as for the ways in which the child views himself, and is regarded by his parents, teachers, and peers. The hyperkinetic syndrome (with or without hyperkinesis) and the minimal brain damage syndrome (with or without evidence of brain damage) are likely to dictate a therapeutic trial of amphetamines or methylphenidate, especially if the child's behavior disrupts the tranquillity of the home or classroom. Children with perceptual motor handicaps were at one time likely to be referred for perceptual retraining. Dyslexia suggests remedial training in reading skills, as does the diagnosis of specific learning disabilities, even though reading disabilities are not synonymous with learning disorders. Sensitive children who are depressed by their school failure or their parents' reaction to their failure are still referred only for individual psychotherapy in some communities. If it is true that indistinguishable groups of children are referred for qualitatively distinct medical and psychologic treatment according to their different diagnoses, then pediatrics, child psychiatry, and child neurology have failed these children badly.

Wender[29] proposed to clean up this Augean stable of "maximal neurological confusion"[13] by formulating a global theory to encompass all the clinical syndromes already listed, as well as an unspecified range of neurotic, psychopathic, and schizophrenic variants of childhood behavior disorders, under the concept of minimal brain dysfunction (MBD). The theory assumes that the heterogeneous childhood disorders are simply individual variations of a common defect in bioamine metabolism, and should therefore respond more or less favorably to specific drugs. There is, however, no persuasive evidence to indicate (and some clinical evidence to the contrary) that all children with MBD constitute a functionally or etiologically homogeneous group. There is, in fact, no evidence (aside from the dramatic improvement of carefully selected children in response to psychoactive drugs) that any of the children have a biochemical defect; and only indirect laboratory evidence to associate variations in bioamine metabolism with changes of behavior. The theory's intent of cutting through scholastic disputes to open up the issue for systematic empirical research is, without question, very attractive. However, if experience can teach us anything, it is more than likely that a concept as vague and global as minimal brain dysfunction will sooner or later be hypostatized, just as similar diagnoses were in the past. The concept MBD will then begin to demand respect in its own right, without ever having been subjected to the tedious work of classification that is necessary to determine the concept's actual significance.

Even at this late date, we may have to settle for a more primitive, empirical strategy, specifying the methods to be used for the neurologic, physiologic, and behavioral examination intercorrelating the various factors in clinically distinct populations, formulating criteria of improvement, and determining how groups of children, who can be distinguished by operational criteria, respond to various treatment programs. In such an effort, it will not be necessary to start again from the beginning. The literature provides some clues about the major categories to be considered, the important variables to be investigated, and the kinds of interventions that are or are not likely to work.

Since our discussion concerns primarily the syndrome of minimal brain damage, it is appropriate to examine in greater detail the neurologic criteria that are commonly used to determine brain damage in children without classical neurologic syndromes.

The general neurologic examination of the child is adequately described. With the single exception of a recent publication by Touwen and Prechtl,[27] however, there is no standardized protocol for the examination of the child with minor neurologic instabilities. Consequently, we still do not know *which* neurologic signs or which combinations of signs are most often associated with particular behavior disorders or developmental delays, but only that two or more unspecified "soft" signs are frequently found in high risk children. We do not know which signs or combinations of signs predict the response to a particular kind of therapeutic intervention.

The observations to be presented below do not pretend to answer the problem of minimal brain damage, its diagnosis, causal determinants, or methods of treatment. Hopefully, they will illustrate that the much maligned term "soft neurologic signs" is no softer than the hard signs of classical neurology, and can be used to good advantage as an indirect index of neurologic dysfunctions in children. Although the study is limited in scope, it may serve as a point of departure for investigating the functional significance of other signs of minor neurologic dysfunction.

CLINICAL STUDY

In a previous publication, we reported the incidence of choreiform movements in normal children and children with demonstrated disturbances of social or educational adaptation.[32] This report concerns the functional significance of choreiform movement in an unselected population of presumably normal children who had not been identified by parents, teachers, or physicians as being in any way abnormal.

Choreiform movements are small jerks of brief duration that occur irregularly and arrhythmically in different muscle groups over the entire body. They are elicited by asking the child to stand with his feet together for a period of 30 seconds, with his head centered, his arms extended, fingers spread as wide apart as possible, and his eyes closed. Choreiform movements are most easily observed and scored by examining the fingers, wrist joints, arms, and shoulders. Prechtl and his associates have found that choreiform movements after the fourth year are significantly associated with a *history* of perinatal distress and minor neurologic signs during the newborn period.[23,24] We found the incidence of choreiform movements to be significantly higher in children with severe psychiatric difficulties (60%–70%), juvenile delinquents (35%), and children with learning difficulties (33%), than in unselected and presumably normal population (11.4%), and three to four times as high in boys as girls.[32]

For this study, we selected a group of 103 boys and 25 girls between the ages of 10 and 12 with unequivocal choreiform movements from the original sample of 1300 normal school children surveyed for choreiform movements, and a control group of 103 boys and 25 girls without choreiform movements who were matched for age, social class, and classroom placement. The incidence of choreiform movements was correlated with the teachers' written reports. Independence of judgment between neurologic signs and school records was guaranteed by the fact that we had no knowledge of the teachers' reports before examining the child, and the teachers were not aware of our study or its results.

In the school system from which the sample was drawn, the teachers make yearly reports about each child's general academic achievement and performance in reading, spelling, and arithmetic; they also describe the child's behavior in the classroom, emphasizing motivation, attention span, peer relations, and social cooperation; and they indicate whether a child has been referred and accepted for psychiatric treatment or

Table 1. Items Scored From Teachers' Comments

Item	Scoring Method	
	Present or Absent	Poor or Good
Academic		
General achievement		x
Reading		x
Mathematics		x
Language		x
Spelling		x
Writing		x
Behavioral		
Motivation		x
Attention span		x
Maturity		x
Work habits		x
Procrastination	x	
Cooperation	x	
Psychoneurologic problem	x	
Underachievement	x	
Hyperactivity	x	
Peer relationships		x
Coordination		x
Speech-hearing problem	x	

other special services. From a preliminary survey of school records, we prepared a checklist of 18 key phrases which occurred most frequently in the teachers' reports. Since the teachers obviously had not written their reports according to our checklist, a "dictionary" of synonyms was prepared and terms such as "works hard," "is conscientious," and "does not exert much effort" were scored as indications of good or poor motivation, while references to concentration and distractibility were scored under attention span (see Table 1).

We anticipated that the relation between minor neurologic signs and behavior disturbances would be influenced significantly by the child's life experience, and that choreiform movements would not be found to correlate with any specific syndrome of behavior disturbances. The twelve items referring to behavior characteristics were, therefore, grouped as one cumulative behavioral rating.

The teachers did not rate every child on every behavior trait on our list, but mentioned only those items in which the child's behavior differed notably in a positive or negative direction. The dictionary was complete enough to encompass all but a few of the comments and there was no need to interpret what the teacher might have meant. Interobserver reliability on all items ranged from 84%–100%, and for items significantly associated with choreiform movements, from 93%–100%.

Records for 95 of the 103 boys with choreiform movements, 75 of the 103 boys without choreiform movements, and for all 50 girls could be traced. The other children had moved before we could examine their records. Raw scores for boys were corrected to compensate for differences in sample size.

RESULTS

Boys

Choreiform movements were independent of social classes, rated by father's occupational classification on the Hollingshead Redlich Scale.[15] There were no significant dif-

Table 2. Cumulative Behavioral Ratings—Boys (Corrected Scores)

Boys	CM+	CM−	χ^2
Favorable reports	5	31	
vs.			27.2*
Unfavorable reports	53	27	
Favorable reports	5	31	
vs.			32.4*
All other reports	90	44	
Unfavorable reports	53	27	
vs.			6.4†
All other reports	42	48	

*$p = 0.001$.
†$p = 0.025$.

ferences in IQ or general academic achievement scores. However, boys with choreiform movements (CM+) had more reading difficulties ($p<0.05$) than boys without choreiform movements (CM−), and more spelling difficulties ($p<0.01$).

Choreiform movements were strongly associated with behavioral disturbances in the classroom. On the cumulative behavioral rating, CM+ boys received significantly fewer *favorable* comments than CM− boys ($p < 0.001$), and significantly more *unfavorable* reports ($p < 0.001$; see Table 2). When the cumulative rating was broken down into subcategories, CM+ boys were less motivated ($p < 0.001$), more immature ($p < 0.05$), had poorer working habits ($p < 0.001$), were less cooperative ($p < 0.01$), less well coordinated ($p < 0.001$), and had more frequent speech and hearing difficulties ($p < 0.01$, see Table 3). The incidence of psychoneurotic disturbances reported by teachers was no different in the two groups, but more CM+ boys had been referred for psychiatric treatment, remedial teaching or other special services, for reasons not specified in the records ($p < 0.025$). The incidence of hyperactivity and poor attention span did *not* differentiate the two groups.

Girls

Choreiform movements were again independent of social class. The IQ scores of CM+ and CM− girls differed significantly, with an 11.5 point difference in mean values ($p < 0.001$). Contrary to our expectations, however, girls *with* choreiform movements received the higher IQ scores. The groups did not differ in general achievement scores or specific academic subjects.

Like the boys, the CM+ girls showed significantly more behavioral disturbances in the classroom. They received fewer favorable reports on the cumulative behavior rating (Table 4) than CM− girls ($p < 0.025$), and significantly more *unfavorable* reports ($p < 0.02$). Girls with choreiform movements were reported to be less mature ($p < 0.01$), to have shorter attention span ($p < 0.01$), and to be less cooperative ($p < 0.01$) (Table 5). We cannot provide a meaningful explanation for the apparent paradox that girls with choreiform movements had relatively higher IQ scores than CM− girls. The finding emphasizes, however, that any generalizations applied to all children that are based on an examination of either males or females alone must be viewed with suspicion (see also Garai and Scheinfeld[12]).

Table 3. Behavioral Items—Boys (Corrected Scores)

Item	CM+	CM−	χ^2
Motivation			
Good	5	19	
Poor	29	11	15.9*
Attention span			
Long	0	16	
Short	1	11	NS
Work habits			
Good	0	20	
Poor	7	8	11.6*
"Maturity"			
Mature	1	9	
Immature	12	12	4.7§
Peer relations			
Good	0	1	
Poor	13	4	NS
Coordination			
Good	2	6	
Poor	11	1	9.2†
			Binomial Test
Cooperation	0	8	†
Hyperactivity	1	0	NS
Psychoneurologic problems	25	11	NS
Underachievement	11	4	NS
Speech-hearing problems	11	1	†
Referred for psychiatric treatment or remedial teaching	15	6	NS
Receiving some psychologic help	12	2	‡

*$p = 0.001$.
†$p = 0.01$.
‡$p = 0.025$.
§$p = 0.05$.

Table 4. Cumulative Behavioral Rating—Girls

Girls	CM+	CM−	χ^2
Favorable reports	4	16	
vs.			8.1*
Unfavorable reports	9	4	
Favorable reports	4	16	
vs.			12.0†
All other reports	21	9	
Unfavorable reports	9	4	
vs.			NS
All other reports	16	21	

*$p = 0.025$.
†$p = 0.01$.

Table 5. Behavioral Items—Girls

Item	CM+	CM−	χ^2
Motivation			
Good	5	5	NS
Poor	10	3	
Attention span			
Long	0	0	*(by Binomial)
Short	11	1	
Work habits			
Good	0	8	10.0†
Poor	2	0	
"Maturity"			
Mature	0	7	*(by Binomial)
Immature	0	0	
Peer relations			
Good	0	3	†
Poor	0	0	
Coordination			
Good	0	3	†
Poor	1	0	
			Binomial Test
Cooperation	0	8	*
Hyperactivity	1	0	NS
Psychoneurologic problems	2	2	NS
Underachievement	3	0	NS
Speech-hearing problems	0	1	NS
Referred for psychiatric treatment or remedial teaching	3	1	NS
Receiving some psychologic help	0	1	NS

*p = 0.01.
†Sample too small.

DISCUSSION

In an unselected population of 10–12-yr-old children attending a public school, 11.4% were found to have one presumptive sign of neurologic dysfunction—the choreiform movement. This sign has been found to correlate with a history of perinatal distress and minor abnormalities in the neonatal period;[22,23] and with learning disorders, juvenile delinquency and severe psychopathology;[14,32] (see, however, Rutter et al.[25] for contrary findings).

The presence of a single neurologic sign in presumably normal children has been reported by other investigators and is generally considered to be of little clinical significance.[14,16,27] Our results indicate that choreiform movements in presumably normal children can identify individuals whose behavior in the classroom differs significantly from that of other children. Had we investigated the functional implications of choreiform movements in a different school system (e.g., a ghetto school), the same behavior disturbances might be significantly associated with learning disorders. Alternatively, different neurologic signs might be associated with other behavior profiles.

Choreiform movements are obviously not pathognomonic of minimal brain damage, minor cerebral dysfunction, or minimal cerebral dysfunction; nor do choreiform movements *cause* severe psychopathology, juvenile delinquency or learning disabilities. It is possible, however, that the behavioral correlates of choreiform movement such as clumsiness, distractibility, and emotional lability make the child a prime target of parental disapproval even before the school years, or that they interfere with the child's schoolwork. The interaction between behavior disturbances commonly associated with choreiform movements and an intolerant social environment may, therefore, predispose the child to one of several well-defined childhood disorders.[14,24]

Because no single sign of minor neurologic dysfunction is pathognomonic of brain damage, most investigators use an array of neurologic signs designed to sample different areas of brain function. Kennard[16] used 21 signs; Hertzig et al.[14] list 11 signs of minor dysfunction and a standard neurologic examination. There is no uniformity in choice of neurologic signs to be used or neurologic functions to be tested. With the exception already mentioned,[27] there is also no standard procedure of examination or interpretation of findings. Results from screening procedures are usually treated as if the different signs were additive—in other words, as if *any* two or more constituted presumptive evidence of minor brain damage regardless of neurophysiologic implications or functional associations. It should, therefore, not come as a great surprise that investigators differ widely on the importance they attribute to minor neurologic signs; or that the invidious term "soft signs" has traveled the same road of hypostatization as the concept of minimal brain damage. When properly defined, the neurologic examination of the child with minor neurologic signs can nevertheless be a powerful tool of research and clinical diagnosis.

Such an examination should distinguish at least between minor pathologic signs that are never observed in normal children, and signs that are normal in children below a certain age, but rated as abnormal in children above a certain age.[1,8,10,27] Beyond this basic twofold classification, the examination should probably also differentiate disturbances in fine and gross motor coordination, delayed lateralization and handedness, lack of sensory integration and a failure in suppression of extraneous movements; each may have qualitatively different implications for the child's social and intellectual adaptation, his academic performance, and his emotional stability. Until the critical studies are carried out, it is premature to conclude that the various signs are equivalent to each other or that the mere number of abnormal signs provides an adequate functional assessment of brain damage.

Systematic classifications of the kind suggested here may begin by comparing the distribution of neurologic signs in unselected and high-risk populations and relating them to behavior categories as we have done. They may begin by identifying behavior disturbances or learning disorders in both unselected and identified populations, and relating these to the distribution of neurologic signs. Efforts to build a rational taxonomy are all the more important today because the treatment of children on a massive basis has become the subject of heated discussions among both lay persons and professionals. Some insist that all children fitting the global concept of MBD "deserve" a therapeutic trial of amphetamines or methylphenidate, no matter how covert or obscure the evidence of brain or neurologic dysfunction may be. The indiscriminate use of amphetamines and methylphenidate without benefit of careful medical screening has raised the justified suspicion among parents, particularly in some inner-city communities, that their children are being subdued pharmacologically because drugs are cheaper than providing an adequate learning environment. Others vigorously oppose the use of any psychoactive drug, and continue to depend exclusively on prolonged psychotherapy for all such children, despite persuasive evidence that in well-selected populations of hyperkinetic children, for example, specific drug therapy can have dramatic beneficial results.[7,18]

SUMMARY

The concept of minimal brain damage has been applied to children without precise definition, and so globally, that it conveys relatively little meaning at present. The concept of MBD runs the same risk as previously applied diagnoses, of being established as a self-evident entity before sufficient empirical evidence has been collated to justify its global use. Since the reasons for selecting one diagnosis in favor of another often have little to do with the child's actual condition, whereas the diagnosis frequently determines what therapeutic intervention will be recommended, a careful classification of objective neurologic signs and related behavior deviations must precede any attempt to unify all relevant signs and symptoms under one global syndrome.

We reported the distribution of a single sign of minor neurologic dysfunction in well-functioning children, and its relation to classroom behavior, to illustrate that even such a questionable measure of neurologic dysfunction may correlate significantly with behavior disturbances in children who would otherwise not come to the attention of the teacher, parent, or pediatrician. The study suggests that the functional significance of individual neurologic signs and of combinations of such signs must be evaluated systematically in both normal children and children already identified as having social and academic difficulties, before any claims can be made for the validity of the minimal brain damage syndrome or any of its identifying features.

REFERENCES

1. Abrams, A. L.: Delayed irregular maturation versus minimal brain injury. Clin. Pediatr. 7:344, 1968.
2. Anderson, W. W.: The hyperkinetic child; a neurological appraisal. Neurology 13:968, 1963.
3. Bakwin, H.: Developmental hyperactivity. Acta Paed. Scand. Suppl. 172, 1967.
4. Bax, M., and MacKeith, R. (Eds.): Minimal Cerebral Dysfunction. Clinics in Developm. Med. 10. London, Spastics Society/Heinemann, 1963.
5. Boshes, B., and Myklebust, H. R.: A neurological and behavioral study of children with learning disorders. Neurology 14:7, 1964.
6. Brenner, M. W., Gilliman, S., Zangwill, O. L., and Farrell, M.: Visuo-motor disability in school children. Br. Med. J. 4:259, 1967.
7. Conners, K., Eisenberg, L., and Barcai, A.: Effect of dextro-amphetamine on children. Arch. Gen. Psychiatry 17:478, 1967.
8. Connolly, K., and Stratton, P.: Developmental changes in associated movements. Dev. Med. Child Neurol. 10:49, 1968.
9. Eisenberg, L.: The management of the hyperkinetic child. Dev. Med. Child Neurol. 8:593, 1966.
10. Fog, E., and Fog, M.: Cerebral inhibition examined by associated movement. *In* Bax, M., and MacKeith, R. (Eds.): Minimal Cerebral Dysfunction. Clinics in Develop. Med. 10. London, Spastics Society/Heinemann, 1963.
11. Frostig, M., and Home, D.: The Frostig Program for Development of Visual Perception. Chicago, Follett, 1964.
12. Garai, J. E., and Scheinfeld, A.: Sex differences in mental and behavioral traits. Genet. Psychol. Monogr. 77:149, 1968.
13. Gomez, B. M. R.: Minimal cerebral dysfunction (maximal neurologic confusion). Clin. Pediatr. 6:589, 1967.
14. Hertzig, M. E., Bortner, M., and Birch, H. G.: Neurologic findings in children educationally designated as "brain damaged." Am. J. Orthopsychiatry 39:437, 1969.
15. Hollingshead, A. B., and Redlich, F. C.: Social Class and Mental Health. New York, Wiley, 1958.
16. Kennard, M.: Value of equivocal signs in neurologic diagnosis. Neurology 10:753, 1960.
17. Laufer, M., and Denhof, E. Hyperkinetic behavior syndrome in children. J. Pediatr. 50:463, 1957.
18. Millichap, J. G.: Drugs in management of

hyperkinetic and perceptually handicapped children. JAMA 206:1527, 1968.

19. Orton, S. T.: Reading, Writing and Speech Problems in Children. New York, Norton, 1937.

20. Paine, R.: Syndromes of minimal cerebral damage. Pediatr. Clin. North Am. 15:779, 1968.

21. Pepper, S.: World Hypotheses. Berkeley, University of California Press, 1946.

22. Prechtl, H. F. R.: The mother-child interaction in babies with minimal brain damage. *In* Foss, B. M. (Ed.): Determinants of Infant Behavior, Vol. II. London, Methuen, 1963, p. 53.

23. —: Prognostic value of neurological signs in the newborn infant. Proc. Royal Soc. Med. 58:3, 1965.

24. —, and Stemmer, C.: The choreiform syndrome in children. Dev. Med. Child. Neurol. 4:119, 1962.

25. Rutter, M., Graham, P., and Birch, H. G.: Interaction between choreiform syndrome reading disability and psychiatric disorders in children of 8–11 years. Dev. Med. Child. Neurol. 8:149, 1966.

26. Strauss, A., and Lehtinen, L. E.: Psychopathology and Education of the Brain-Injured Child. New York, Grune & Stratton, 1947.

27. Touwen, B. C. H., and Prechtl, H. F. R.: Neurological Examination of the Child with Minor Nervous Dysfunction. Clinics in Developm. Med. 38. London, Spastics International Publications, Heinemann, 1970.

28. Walker, M.: Perceptual, coding, visuomotor and spatial difficulties and their neurological correlates. Dev. Med. Child. Neurol. 7:543, 1965.

29. Wender, P. H.: Minimal Brain Dysfunction in Children. New York, Wiley, 1971.

30. Werner, H., and Strauss, A.: Pathology of figure-background relation in the child. J. Abnorm. Soc. Psychol. 36:236, 1941.

31. Werry, J. S.: Studies on the hyperactive child. IV. An empirical analysis of the minimal brain dysfunction syndrome. Arch. Gen. Psychiatry 19:9, 1968.

32. Wolff, P. H., and Hurwitz, I. The choreiform syndrome. Dev. Med. Child. Neurol. 8:160, 1966.

SUBJECT INDEX

Minimal Cerebral Dysfunction in Children

Acquired behavior, neuropathology of after asphyxia, 26-32
Amphetamines, neurophysiologic response to in MBD treatment, 13-14
Asphyxia neonatorum, specific neuropathology of in rhesus monkeys, 20-24
Auditory evoked response, latencies and amplitude of in MBD children, 42-45

Behavior, adaptive development of following asphyxia in rhesus monkeys, 24-26
Behavioral categories, selection of for observation in MBD "free-field" observation, 90-92
Behavioral disorder
  genetic issues in MBD in children, 5-15
  and MBD in children, 81-92
  neurologic signs of, 109-114
Benzedrine (D,L amphetamine), in treatment of hyperactivity syndrome, 10-11
Blood, lead levels in, 48-49
Brain dysfunction, methylphenidate treatment response and, 35-46
Brain function, impairment by lead poisoning, 47-53
Brain mechanisms, analysis of in MBD children, 81-84
Brain structure, memory deficits and asphyxia, 28-29

Central nervous system, delayed maturation in MBD children, 35-46
Childhood MBD, psychiatric problems and relatives, 6-7
Choreiform movements, in MBD children, 108-113
Cognitive functions, intercorrelation analysis of in learning disabilities, 63-68
Cortical responses, audio-evoked experiment, 42-45

Delta-aminolavulenic acid dehydrase, inhibition by lead, 48-49, 51
Dexedriene (D-amphetamine), in treatment of hyperactivity syndrome, 10-11
Dextroamphetamine, in hyperkinetic syndrome, 100-101
Discriminate analysis, and identification of learning-disability children, 68

Educational achievement, and learning disability diagnosis, 62-63
Electrocardiogram
  abnormalities and MBD treatment response, 35-46
  in identification of children with learning disabilities, 59
  study in learning disability diagnosis, 59, 70-76
Emotional liability. *See* Hyperkinetic syndrome
Environment, structure of and MBD children, 88-89
Environmental manipulation, in treatment of hyperkinetic syndrome, 100
Epidemiologic data, for MBD, 5-8
Etiology, of hyperkinetic syndrome, 98-99

"Free-field" observation, in MBD children, 85-92

Genetics, role of factors in MBD, 5-8
Genetic studies, of MBD, 11-14

Hyperkinesis and MBD, 106
Hyperkinetics, in hyperkinetic syndrome, 99-100
Hyperkinetic syndrome, 95-102
  clinical description, 95-96
  etiology, 98-99
  hyperkinesis in, 99-100
  pathologic process of, 97-98
  prevalence of, 96-97
  treatment, 100-102

Intelligence, and mental retardation, 8-9

Language, and learning disability diagnosis, 62-63
Lead
  age and vulnerability to, 51
  blood levels of, 48-49
  environmental sources of, 51-52
  tooth levels of, 49-51
Lead poisoning, neurologic implications of, 47-53
Learning, discrimination and asphyxia, 29-32
Learning ability, emotional adjustment and, 63
  intercorrelation analysis of integration of cognitive function of, 63-68
  locomotor coordination and, 63
  social maturity and, 63

SUBJECT INDEX

Learning disability
  defined, for disability study, 57
  identification and diagnosis in children with, 55–77
  See also Hyperkinetic syndrome
Learning quotient, definition of, 57
Locomotor development, adaptive behavior developed after asphyxia, 25

Memory, asphyxia and, 28
  response after neonatal asphyxia, 26–28
Mental ability, in learning disability diagnosis, 57, 62
Mental disorder, genetic effect on, 8–9
Methylphenidate (Ritalin)
  in treatment of hyperactivity syndrome, 11
  in MBD treatment, 35–46
Methylphenidate, in hyperkinetic syndrome treatment, 100–101
Minimal brain damage
  diagnosis of, 106–107
  electrocardiogram and methylphenidate treatment for, 35–46
  functional implications of, 105–114
  pharmacogenetic analysis of, 10–15
  sex difference in frequency of, 9–10
  syndrome, 106
  See also Hyperkinetic syndrome
Minimal cerebral dysfunction, in children, 30–31
  See also Hyperkinetic syndrome, Minimal brain damage

Neonatal asphyxia, and MCD, comparison of disorders, 30–31
Neurologic assessment, of children with MBD, 80–84
Neurologic dysfunction, methylphenidate treatment and, 35–46
Neurologic impairment, by lead poisoning, 47–53
Neurologic profile, of children with MBD, 82–83

Neurologic signs, relation to behavioral disturbances, 109–114
Neurologic study
  in learning disability diagnosis, 59–60
  in learning disability, findings tabulated, 72–75
Neurology, criteria used to determine brain damage, 107–108
Neuropathology, of asphyxia in rhesus monkeys, 21–24
Neurophysiologic responses, to amphetamines in children, 13

Ophthalmologic study, in learning disability diagnosis, 55–59, 68–69

Pathologic process, of hyperkinetic syndrome, 97–99
Prenatal conditions, influence on MBD, 19
Psychoeducational study, in learning disability diagnosis procedure, 51–58, 60–62
Psychoeducational tests, discriminant analysis, 68
Psychologic impairment, by lead poisoning, 47–53
Psychosocial adaptation, factors affecting, 1, 2
Psychotherapy, and hyperkinetic syndrome treatment, 101–102
Pupillography, electronic, and hyperactivity in children, 12–13

Response performance, asphyxia and, 28
Ritalin. *See* Methylphenidate

Sex difference, in MBD frequency, 9–10

Tricyclic antidepressant imipramine, in treatment of hyperactivity syndrome, 11

Underachievers, and learning disability, 55–77

Visual depth perception, adaptive behavior after asphyxia, 24, 75
Visual placing, adaptive behavior developed after asphyxia, 24–25

Contributors

Eisenberg, Leon, M.D., Chief, Psychiatric Services, Massachusetts General Hospital, and Professor of Psychiatry, Harvard Medical School, Boston, Mass.

Faro, Maria D., Ph.D., Assistant Professor of Rehabilitation Medicine, New York University Medical Center, New York, N. Y.

Hurwitz, Irving, Ph.D., Assistant Professor of Psychiatry, Harvard Medical School, Boston, Mass.

Kalverboer, A. F., Ph.D., Department of Developmental Neurology, University Hospital, Groningen, The Netherlands.

Myklebust, Helmer R., Ed.D., Professor, College of Education, University of Illinois at Chicago Circle, Chicago, Ill.

Needleman, Herbert L., M.D., Assistant Professor of Psychiatry, Harvard Medical School, Boston, Mass.

O'Malley, John E., M.D., Major, M.C. United States Army; Chief, Outpatient Psychiatry, Madigan General Hospital, Tacoma, Wash.

Omenn, Gilbert S., M.D., Ph.D., Assistant Professor of Medicine, Division of Medical Genetics, University of Washington School of Medicine, Seattle, Wash.

Richmond, Julius B., M.D., Professor of Child Psychiatry and Human Development, and Professor and Chairman, Department of Preventive and Social Medicine, Harvard Medical School; Psychiatrist-in-Chief, Children's Hospital Medical Center; and Director, Judge Baker Guidance Center, Boston, Mass.

Satterfield, James H., M.D., Director of Research, Andrew Norman Research Center, Gateways Hospital, and Associate Clinical Professor of Psychiatry, University of California, Los Angeles, Calif.

Sechzer, Jeri A., Ph.D., Associate Professor of Psychiatry, Edward W. Bourne Behavioral Research Laboratory, The New York Hospital-Cornell Medical Center, White Plains, N. Y.

Touwen, B. C. L., M.D., Department of Developmental Neurology, University Hospital, Groningen, The Netherlands.

Walzer, Stanley, M.D., Assistant Professor of Psychiatry, Harvard Medical School, Boston, Mass.

Windle, William F., Ph.D., Research Professor, Denison University, Granville, Ohio.

Wolff, Peter H., M.D., Professor of Psychiatry, Harvard Medical School, Boston, Mass.

Randall Library – UNCW
RJ506.M4 W34   NXWW
Walzer / Minimal cerebral dysfunction in children;

3049001780997